I'LL GIVE YOU A DAISY A DAY

An Anthology of Funeral Sermons and Articles On Death

Edited by Victor A. Myers

I'LL GIVE YOU A DAISY A DAY

Grateful acknowledgment is made to Kathie Baker, Ann Hetrick, Louise Forsch of Akron University, and Nancy Myers who assisted by transcribing, typing and proofing this manuscript.

0900/ISBN 0-89536-324-0
PRINTED IN U.S.A.

DEDICATED TO

Reverend Charles Edgar and Clara Elaine Liebegott
and
Members of:
St. Paul Lutheran — Akron, Ohio
Trinity Lutheran — Kent, Ohio
. . . two grandparents and two congregations
who have contributed to my "life-story" by
sharing their understanding of "God's Story."

TABLE OF CONTENTS

NOTES ON THE CONTRIBUTORS

DR. FRANK EFIRD is the pastor of Holy Trinity Lutheran Church, Akron, Ohio, and former campus pastor at the University of Wisconsin.

GEORGE W. GAISER is a clergyman of the American Lutheran Church, and the campus pastor in the Lutheran Campus Ministry program at Kent State University, Kent, Ohio. He is a part-time instructor in the Honors and Experimental College at KSU.

HERBERT S. GARNES, III is pastor of St. Jacob Lutheran Church in North Canton, Ohio. He serves as District Coordinator for the Canton District of the Ohio Synod, Lutheran Church in America.

DR. A. ROGER GOBBEL is Dean and Professor of Functional Theology at the Lutheran Theological Seminary in Gettysburg, Pennsylvania.

DR. DONALD R. HEIGES is President Emeritus of the Lutheran Theological Seminary in Gettysburg, Pennsylvania.

S. CYRIL HURNYAK is associate pastor and director of music at St. John Lutheran Church, Lancaster, New York.

HOBERT B. JOHNSON is the pastor at the Kent United Methodist Church, Kent, Ohio, and a former United Methodist Missionary in South Korea.

FRANK A. KANTZ serves as Lutheran Campus Pastor at the Indiana University of Pennsylvania in Indiana, Pennsylvania.

JOHN KINDSVATTER is the pastor of St. John Lutheran Church, Philadelphia, Pennsylvania.

A. DONALD MAIN serves as pastor of Trinity Lutheran Church, Altoona, Pennsylvania. He serves as Dean of the Altoona District of the Central Pennsylvania Synod, Lutheran Church in America.

CARL W. MANGOLD is pastor of Reformation Lutheran Church, Eastlake, Ohio. He serves as District Coordinator for the Cleveland District of the Ohio Synod, Lutheran Church in America.

THEODORE C. MAYER is the former Akron District Superintendent of the United Methodist Church.

RICHARD F. MICHAEL is pastor of the Lutheran Church of the Holy Spirit in Lancaster, Pennsylvania.

VICTOR A. MYERS serves as pastor of Trinity Lutheran Church, Kent, Ohio. He serves as District Coordinator for the Akron District of the Ohio Synod, Lutheran Church in America. He is a part-time instructor in the Honors and Experimental college at KSU.

ALLEN MYRICK is pastor of the United Church of Christ, Kent, Ohio. He was formerly a theological teacher and administrator at the Federal Theological Seminary of Southern Africa.

THOMAS N. ROGERS is pastor of First Lutheran Church, Donnelsville, Ohio, and serves as District Coordinator for the Springfield District of the Ohio Synod, Lutheran Church in America.

JOHN P. SELTZER is co-pastor of Bethany and Zion Lutheran Churches in Niagara Falls, New York.

DONALD W. SHILLING is a clergyman of the United Methodist Church and serves as pastor on the staff of United Christian Ministries at Kent State University, Kent, Ohio. He teaches a course on "Death and Dying" in the Honors and Experimental College at KSU.

STANLEY C. SNEERINGER is pastor of St. Timothy Lutheran Church, Mansfield, Ohio.

DR. ROBERT W. STACKEL serves as Executive Director of the "Love Compels Action/World Hunger Appeal" for the Lutheran Church in America.

BETH E. WIESEMAN is pastor of St. John Lutheran Church, Sulphur Springs, Ohio and St. Paul Lutheran Church, North Robinson, Ohio.

C. KING WYNKOOP is associate pastor of Emmanuel Lutheran Church in New Philadelphia, Ohio.

GERALD J. WISE is Director of Music and organist at Trinity Lutheran, Kent, Ohio. He has published a number of compositions for organ and chorus.

Introduction

THE FUNERAL SERMON AS "A STORY"
Victor A. Myers

Once upon a time, an assortment of folks huddled together in a church lounge. An attractive college student undertaking a nursing program; arthritic octogenarians walking with the aid of canes; a young man with leukemia; a middle-aged woman, who, because of her battle with cancer, could have been a model during the Middle Ages for a woodcut depicting death; grieving young parents whose "swinging" life-style was shattered by the reality that their five-year-old son was felled by a semitrailer; and a host of curious and confused . . . they had come together for a seminar on "death and dying." These unique children of God were asked to write and then share some of their ideas and feelings about their own funeral service, including the funeral sermon.

"I don't want the pastor to give a flattering eulogy," commented one participant.

"I don't know what you mean by eulogy," another member said hesitantly. "But I do know that my mother's funeral service was quite cold and harsh because the minister made no mention of my mother in his sermon. I felt little comfort because he could have been talking about anyone. I cried for days."

"Yes, I know that empty feeling," the attractive nurse interjected. "All the minister did during my grandmother's funeral sermon was quote one Bible passage after another. He droned on as if he had given that same sermon at every funeral service."

"That sounds similar to the sermon preached at my grandfather's funeral," blurted a high school coed. "The sermon was very vague and general. It made me feel as if the preacher thought my grandfather was

'Everyman.' He wasn't! He was very special to us. He was certainly unique. He is the one who really helped open up my faith in God. In fact, I just wanted to jump up and yell, 'stop!' I do not think the minister really knew my grandfather."

This story of the seminar does not close by suggesting that "everyone lived happily ever after." Instead, this story reminds us that "the ending" is written every time a funeral sermon is prepared. Moreover, these candid expressions about the funeral sermon bring into focus the dilemma: 1) Lay people do articulate two extreme opinions regarding the composition and message of the funeral sermon. 2) These two views are part of the reality confronting the sensitive pastor on each occasion when he or she is called to deliver a funeral sermon.

More succinctly stated, the dilemma simply involves answering a question: Is the funeral sermon a eulogy or merely a string of biblical quotations?

Yet, is this *really* the dilemma? Should the funeral sermon be envisioned as merely an "either/or" choice between eulogy and a string of biblical quotations and an exposition? I think not! More appropriately, the funeral sermon should be envisioned as "both/and," that is, both a eulogy and a message containing the Word of God.

When comprising both eulogy and a message revealing the Word of God, what then is the center and format of the funeral sermon?

I propose that the funeral sermon be approached, planned, written, and delivered as "a story." In order to reveal the reasons why I suggest this proposition of the "funeral sermon as story," I would like to share an assortment of random reflections which have their genesis in a variety of experiences which make up a portion of my life story. These reflections can be summarized as follows:

1) On one occasion, I participated in a seminar led by Rabbi Abraham Heschel. After an initial presentation, a student posed a rather profound moral question. There was a pause in the dialogue between student and teacher. Then the rabbi looked at the student, smiled, and replied, "My friend, let me tell you a story."

2) Like Rabbi Heschel, Dr. Jacob Myers, Professor of Old Testament Study at the Lutheran Theological Seminary in Gettysburg, Pennsylvania, impacted my life by demonstrating that the telling of a story is a particularly unique way of dealing with ultimate issues. A story focuses attention on deeds not doctrine, on concrete reality not some abstraction. As Dr. Myers reminded us so often: "Hebrew scriptures speak to us of God by telling us a story. We do not hear theologians arguing about propositions of an ontological or theological nature. Instead, we learn stories about kings and queens, court intrigue, friendships, temple prostitutes, a drunken sailor, a prophet whose wife is unfaithful, golden calves, and genealogies."

3) What is "The Story?" Robert Jenson, Professor of Theology at the Lutheran Seminary in Gettysburg, would suggest that it is the fact that "God came to speech in Jesus Christ."

4) "The Story," as the Christian understands it, involves three ingredients: a) The Central story of Jesus, the Christ. This is God's story. b) My "personal life story" is important, especially as it relates to God's Story. The combination of God's Story and my life story provides the content of my witness. c) My "neighbor's story" is likewise important. Evangelism is my telling Jesus' story in relationship to my life story, in a way which is relevant to my neighbor's story.

5) John Vannorsdall, Chaplain at Yale University, served as my Chaplain Intern Supervisor at Gettysburg College. On those occasions when we would critique

sermons, "JV" would stress: "Vic, learn to use images effectively! People listening to you do not have a sermon text or a biblical text before them to read." He went on to say that "folks must hear crisp images. Images create pictures which help them know what a Bible passage means to you, their pastor. A distinct image will help them long remember the point you wish to make. Work equally hard on Exegesis *and* the development of an appropriate image. It will take careful and exhaustive thinking. But when you share a good image in a sermon, you will be able to sense that folks are longing to hear more."

6) The late H. Grady Davis, author of *Design for Preaching*, made a lasting impact on both my life and preaching during the year he served as guest lecturer at the Lutheran Seminary in Gettysburg. He, too, impressed on me the necessity of learning how to use stories. Here is a sample of his notions about the value of stories in preaching (taken from class notes, notes from private conversations, and tape recordings of discussions):

A) "Too often we think we must always quote Scripture. Have we forgotten that Jesus told parables? Learn from Jesus' example. As a superb teacher, Jesus was keenly aware that folks learn from stories. Even a small child remembers stories."

B) "Exercise painstaking care in writing and then telling a good story! And by a good story, I mean one that catches the imagination of the congregation. Get people 'caught up' in the story. Be ever so careful to show folks how the story fits in to the story of Jesus and how it relates to their every day experiences."

C) "Develop some sensitivity so that you can identify stories as you share in the everyday, ordinary events of your parishioners. But, when reciting those stories, do not fall short by failing to link them with the story of Jesus in the biblical text."

D) "So, you want to be a storyteller? Well, then, you will have to study the biblical text. You will have to study it even when you have reached a point when you think you can study it no longer. Coupled with saturating your life with the text, you will have to develop your insights about parishioners. What makes them cry and laugh? Why are they hurting? What do they need to hear? What can they understand? How will you help them grow so that they can, at some point, grasp what now they may not be able to grasp?"

7) H. Grady Davis also shared fresh ideas about biblical preaching in the context of the funeral service.

A) "Biblical preaching, including the funeral sermon, is proclamation of the God Story. And God's Story is held up to remind the grieving community of believers and non-believers of its identity and purpose before God. Equally important, we must share the implications of that identity and purpose for life in terms of the past-present-future development of their individual life stories."

B) "The pastor, during the funeral, is the link between the biblical text(s) and the community of friends which will uncover a new identity and be confronted by the biblical text(s)."

C) "Funeral sermons, while telling a story, must also remind people of sin . . . their sin . . . and the forgiveness received because of *both* the Cross and Resurrection. That is God's Story; and it helps us all deal with and make sense of our life experiences."

These random reflections are meant to serve as a catalyst for further exploration into the nature of the funeral sermon.

In addition, a careful scrutiny of the random reflections unveils a subtle point: the notations about funeral sermons have been influenced by individuals who shared, with me, their own unique life story and understanding of God's Story. Individuals made an impact on my life and faith! Indeed, the inventory tells a story about individuals who have affected this paper.

In a similar fashion, when planning, developing, and writing the funeral sermon, one needs to be conscious of the individual. To focus thinking, ask some essential questions: How has the life story of the individual made an impact on my life? How has this individual's faith fostered new thoughts about my faith? How has the fusion of this person's life story and his understanding of God's Story been influential to me? to others? to the congregation? to the community? What concrete stories from this person's life might provide a deeper understanding of an appropriate, comforting biblical text for the occasion of the funeral?

But how does one begin to answer such questions and in turn develop a "funeral story"?

As you begin the task of weaving the threads of the individual's life story, God's Story, and how an understanding of God's Story has influenced the individual, into a rich, colorful tapestry that forms the "funeral story," this planning method will prove helpful:

BEGIN IMMEDIATELY TO: 1. *Look around* and begin to develop a sensitivity for "stories" in everyday life. 2. *Read* good literature to become familiar with exemplary stories; to discover what it means to be an effective storyteller. 3. *Practice writing* and rewriting stories.

BEFORE WRITING THE FUNERAL SERMON: 1. *Actively listen to the family.* Determine what stories impacted their lives. What seem to be the "most talked about" events? What unique elements of this person's life story have been influential to this family? 2. Seek to uncover insights as a result of such questions as: How has this individual contributed to your spiritual development? How has his/her life story added to a family story? a community story? a congregational story? Under what circumstances did the individual come to a clear understanding of God's Story? 3. *Consider appropriate, comforting Bible passages.* Look at the significant stories and seek to discover how the individual's life story has been impacted by a particular biblical passage (or passages). What texts have you used with this person during times of crisis? Would that particular text, in the context of telling the individual's life story, be of comfort to the family? Can an appropriate image be developed as you listen to both God's Story and the individual's story? How might the person's life story illuminate the message contained in the appropriate biblical text?

PREPARING THE FUNERAL SERMON TEXT: 1. *Be realistic,* avoid telling merely a "glowing" life story; after all, life is not all glory. The cross and suffering and disappointment are elements in any story depicting human life. 2. *Consider the total "funeral story" text.* Does the final text comfort and at the same time confront the listeners with the reality that God's Story adds meaning and purpose to their own life story?

The sermons which follow provide a variety of illustrations of how pastors in diverse settings have used the funeral sermon as "a story."

While the sermons contained in this volume are 'models' of the funeral sermon as "a story," they are *not* printed to simply provide an easy prototype which is adapted to any situation by merely changing names. Each pastor much wrestle with the Word of God in his or her own unparalleled setting/situation.

Easter, 1977
Kent, Ohio

STORIES OF

INFANTS AND YOUTH

A Lifetime Of One Day

Victor A. Myers

SETTING: *This meditation was written for the graveside service of an infant girl who was given a lifetime of one day. The infant's parents and grandparents had very little contact with the church.*

TEXT: *For I am certain of this: neither death nor life, no angel, no prince, nothing that exists, nothing still to come, not any power, or height or depth, nor any created thing, can ever come between us and the love of God made visible in Christ Jesus our Lord.* [Romans 8:38-39, Jerusalem Bible]

Sunday I stood dressed in a hospital gown at Children's Hospital. I had come to baptize your daughter, Shannon Amy. I placed my fingertips, wet with water, gently and tenderly on her tiny, warm forehead. During that moment of Baptism, I could feel the tears. Her tiny, two pound form became blurred by the mist in my eyes. Such a frail young life. Such a beautiful child of God. And I thought I could detect a little of her mother's red hair. Shannon stirred, just a little, as I pronounced the blessing.

For a moment I stood silently. As I gazed through blurred eyes at Shannon, I wondered. I wondered what life would bring her way. I wondered what would become of this infant. What, in years to come, would make her cry and laugh? How would she feel about God? about life?

Later that same afternoon, Shannon's life brought us together as a family. She united us: Lachlan and Debbie, Mr. and Mrs. Truex, Mr. and Mrs. McIntosh. She united us in a hospital room to pray for God's help. To ask for God's peace . . . for our joy was now mixed with some anxiety and dread about what the future would bring.

Then, suddenly, one day had become a lifetime. And for whatever the reason, God in his wisdom gave Shannon Amy a lifetime of one day. Yet, honestly, when an infant is given but a day of life — no easy words comfort us.

Our only hope, I believe, comes from those timeless promises of God! One such message of hope was spoken by Jesus: "It is not the will of my Father who is in heaven that one of these little ones should perish." (Matthew 18:14) I believe that!

Also, I believe we receive comfort from the promise contained in Shannon's Baptism. In that sacramental moment, God was present, reminding us that Shannon and each of us is his child. God would care for Shannon because he loved her. Because of the love given us in Christ, Shannon, through her Baptism, became a Child of God . . . without any merit on her part.

Also in Baptism, God reminds us that it is not how long a person lives that matters. Rather, it is for what a person lives. Every life has a purpose.

Shannon's lifetime of one day had a purpose.

I would suggest that through Shannon's Baptism, God once again reminded us that we are his, because of our Baptism. Each of us is indeed a child of God. Because of the mark of Baptism on her frail forehead, Shannon lived her lifetime of one day as God's! Perhaps, then, this tiny angel's purpose was to remind us of our Baptism and that we, too, are God's . . . and that we need to discover in our individual lives what we are living for.

Perhaps, too, this tiny angel's purpose was to remind us that we must live life one day at a time . . . one day at a time, with God. For just as Shannon's life was sacred to God, so too is the life he has given to us. How will you live this one day for God?

But equally important, Shannon's life and Baptism are a reminder to us that nothing can separate us from God. Shall a lifetime of one day separate us from God's love? Shall our heartache and sorrow as we stand at this graveside? No! "In all these things we are more than conquerors through him who loved us. For I am persuaded that neither death nor life, nor angels, nor governments, nor powers, nor things present, nor things to come, nor height nor depth, nor any creature shall be able to separate us from the love of God which is in Christ Jesus our Lord!" (Romans 8:38-39) Nothing shall separate Shannon from the love of God poured out richly to her at that moment of Baptism!

May these promises give us hope. Now. Forever. Amen.

LET US PRAY: O God, we pray for your help to accept what we cannot understand. We pray for your help in understanding what we find hard to accept. And in the quiet of this summer afternoon, sustain us in the hope of Easter Grant to Shannon a new beginning with you . . . where your peace reigns and where there is no more sorrow. Prod us in the fresh discovery that it is for you that we live . . . one day at a time. And now confident of your compassion, we commend ourselves to your care, until we with Shannon Amy McIntosh share wholeness and newness of Life in the Kingdom to come. Amen.

He Took Them In His Arms

John Kindsvatter

SETTING: *William Leaf died in an automobile accident. At the time of his death he was seven years old. The parents donated William's body to a medical school for the purpose of scientific study.*

TEXT: *And they were bringing children to him, that he might touch them; and the disciples rebuked them. But when Jesus saw it he was indignant, and said to them, "Let the children come to me, do not hinder them; for to such belongs the kingdom of God. Truly, I say to you, whoever does not receive the kingdom of God like a child shall not enter it." And he took them in his arms and blessed them, laying his hands upon them. [Mark 10:13-16, NEB]*

We come together this day to share Bob and Linda's grief in the death of their son, William. We support the entire family at this moment. We embrace them at this most difficult time in their lives.

Mark tells of a day in Jesus' life when children, in all of their impatient excitement, crowded around Jesus to touch him. One problem: the large number of adults standing around Jesus, listening to him. Children have a special way of taking over and, with that in mind, we can picture the children crawling between the adults' legs, or sliding in and through the people in order to get closer to Jesus.

Adults have a way of becoming proper with age, and sometimes brittle with their patience, uncomfortable, and even angry when children interfere with their important concentrations. Nevertheless, children have priorities like anyone else, and in the Gospel of Mark, they were persistently maneuvering their way through the crowd when some of the disciples grabbed them — what we call today "crowd control" — and talked to the children. The disciples then pushed the children away from Jesus.

Children are people. Children are God's creation. Jesus was angry with the disciples, and told them that they must themselves be more like children to live in God's kingdom. Jesus then took the children in his arms. He blessed them with his love.

This is my picture of God's love for William.

This is my picture of Jesus' ministry: his arms around William because of the love they share together in God's love.

God is the common element in our world, in our lives as individuals and our lives collectively as a society. God is the love through which we have life. Just as William was conceived in love, he died in the same, yet stronger-by-seven-years-love that now means so much hurt for Bob and Linda. But we know in their deep sadness that God is speaking to them and letting them know that his love, which gave form and substance to William in this world, continues now with William because he is most certainly with God. This is our faith, that the love God uses to create life keeps us with him.

The good news in Jesus Christ (that we share with one another this afternoon) is that God and William have always been together and always will be together. Like William, we have the same oneness: God and us. We are together in Jesus Christ. Nothing in this world changes that beautiful message.

"For I am sure that neither death, nor life, nor angels, nor things present, nor things to come, nor powers, nor anything else in creation, will be able to separate us from the love of God in Christ Jesus our Lord." (Romans 8:38-39, RSV)

Bob and Linda were saying Sunday that, when William died, a little of all of us died. This is true, because all of us are emptier without William and everything in his life that he shared with us. At the same time, we are all richer in our lives and are better people because we knew William and his life. Seven years is not a long time from our perspective, and yet, Bob and Linda will never experience another seven years like William again. They are very special years indeed!

And for us, as friends, we do not know what those seven years will mean in the remainder of our lives. We are certainly aware of what William's life has meant to us in the past. He will continue to be important for all of us in the future.

For this we thank William.

For this we thank God.

Death always makes us realize how important life is: that minutes are crucial and full of potential. And in time, Bob, Linda, their families and we, their friends, will feel joy realizing that the pain belongs to us and not William. We will realize, too, that while we miss William and feel the hurt of his loss, his seven years were happiness and joy . . .

. . . for him,

. . . for Bob and Linda,

. . . for the families,

. . . and for us, his friends.

One joy for William was singing a Swedish hymn. Hear those words:

> Children of the heavenly Father
> Safely in his bosom gather;
> Nestling bird nor star in heaven
> Such a refuge e'er was given.
>
> God his own doth tend and nourish,
> In his holy courts they flourish.
> From all evil things he spares them,
> In his mighty arms he bears them.

Neither life nor death shall ever
From the Lord his children sever;
Unto them his grace he showeth,
And their sorrows all he knoweth.

Though he giveth or he taketh,
God his children ne'er forsaketh,
His the loving purpose solely
To preserve them pure and holy.

God's love in Jesus Christ cares and keeps William with him. This is God's promise for us, too. This is our hope. With God's love, this can be our joy, in the Name of the Father, and of the Son, and of the Holy Spirit. Amen.

Come To Me

Dr. Frank Efird

SETTING: *This sermon was preached at the funeral of a fourteen year old girl who died with cancer shortly before she was to be confirmed.*

TEXT: *Come to me, all who labor and are heavy laden, and I will give you rest.* [Matthew 11:28, RSV]

Today, the body of Kris is in this church for the last time. It rests here before the altar. She had looked forward to being confirmed at this altar with her classmates. Death struck her down. Though she was not confirmed, today she graduates from the church below to the church above, from the church militant to the church triumphant. We welcome all of you today to her graduation.

Above the altar, where Kris would have been confirmed, you see a statue of Christ. His arms are wide open. Looking at his face, we are reminded of his words, "Come to me, all who labor and are heavy laden, and I will give you rest." (Matthew 11:28, RSV)

Today, Christ addresses these words to Kris and to her family.

I. Jesus addresses these words to Kris.

"Come to me, Kris. You are a learner who will still be learning." Kris was a student. She came regularly to catechetical classes until the beginning of her illness. She was an avid learner. She was eager to know more about Jesus Christ and his love.

God is so great and his Son so magnificent that all of eternity will be a learning experience, of knowing more and more about the heavenly Father and Jesus and his love. Kris was a student who is still learning. Confirmation will be her experience now. Forever.

"Come to me, Kris. You are a worshiper who is still worshiping." Kris regularly came to worship and glorify God in this place. But today, her church letter of transfer has been sent to a new congregation: the heavenly communion of saints. She glorified God here; she will glorify him in eternity. She sang his praises here; she shall sing them in eternity.

"Come to me, Kris. You are a servant still serving."

"Therefore are they before the throne of God, and serve him day and night within his temple." (Revelation 7:15, RSV)

Kris had only fourteen years to serve God at Trinity. But it is not the number of years you have in your life; rather it is the life you put in your years that is important. Kris put a lot of serving in her short life. The "rest" of eternity will not be inactivity but joyful service of God.

II. Jesus Christ addresses these words to her loved ones. To you he says, "Come to me."

The Christ who addresses you with open arms knows your pain. "Surely, he has borne our griefs and carried our sorrows." (Isaiah 53:4) The compassionate Christ is acquainted with your grief. He wept at the tomb of his friend. He suffered gross physical pain on the cross. He knew mental affliction. He cried amidst his suffering, "My God, my God, why hast thou forsaken me?" (Matthew 27:46, KJV)

There are certain mysteries of life Jesus did not explain, such as, why it is that some people live to be quite old, others die young. He died at thirty-three. But, in the way he bore the tragedy of death, and in the way he rose from death through the work of his Father, he revealed a power that is stronger than the mystery: that God can bring life out of death!

He offers a dynamic grace that can turn what appear to be minus marks into plus marks. Though in the eyes of his disciples his demise on the cross seemed like a minus mark, God turned it into a plus mark. He turned what appeared to be tragedy into triumph.

It is probably in times like these that we think most deeply on the meaning and purpose of life. We learn more fully the meaning of the words, "My grace is sufficient for you." (2 Corinthians 12:9, RSV) And certainly, our sympathies are intensified for those who suffer. We become members of the "fellowship of those who have accepted pain."

Children are God's gifts to us. Children like Kris add joy to our homes. They create great memories. There is a sense in which they are on loan to us. Sooner or later we know in this world we shall be separated. But if we have deep faith as Kris had in Jesus, we know, through the power of the Resurrection, we shall be together around him.

How do you, her family, stay close to Kris? Her Lord has welcomed her to himself. She is with him. To stay near Kris, stay close to Christ.

A university professor and his wife took their children out west. One day, they visited a large cave which reminded one of a cathedral, with stalactites like huge organ pipes in front. Gradually the lights went off as a quartet sang, "Rock of Ages cleft for me, let me hide myself in thee." When the music ended, there was a dead silence and absolute darkness. The little boy grabbed his sister's hand and said, "I'm scared!"

She whispered, "Don't be afraid Johnny, there's a man around who knows how to turn the lights back on again."

We can trust God. For his Son in the darkness of death, he turned the lights back on again. For us, who sit in darkness, he makes his light shine, the light of hope, the light of power, the light of eternal life.

Let us this day trust in him who says, "Come to me." For the Light of the world turns the lights back on for Kris, for you, forever.

STORIES OF

HUMAN SUFFERING

I'll Give You A Daisy A Day

Victor A. Myers

SETTING: *This homily was preached at the graveside service of a cousin who died following a lengthy battle with the ravages of cancer.*

TEXTS: Romans 8:38-39
2 Corinthians 4:7-12

On this morning, I would like to share a simple thought.

You in this place are, with me, aware that Florence or 'Bus' (as some of us nicknamed her) was quite fond of daisies . . . fresh, golden, glistening daisies.

As a lover of daisies, Bus would have loved a current popular song entitled: "I'll Give You A Daisy a Day, Dear." It is a song which tells of the love of a man for a woman. In their youth, the man picked from the green fields a daisy for his lady-fair. He gave her one daisy each day. In the days of growing children, he would present to her each night a golden yellow and white daisy. Even in the twilight of his years, he could be found slowly walking to the hillside cemetery . . . continuing to give her a daisy a day.

I would now simply suggest that Bus gave to each of us in this place a daisy a day.

To some or all of us she gave the "Daisy of Laughter." Perhaps she gave us this daisy on our grey days and sad. Perhaps she caught sight of our tears and our worry. Then, with the twinkling of an eye, she would tell a story, and worries would melt and soon disappear. Laughter and a fresh measure of joy would be ours!

To some or all of us she gave the "*Daisy of Insight and Wisdom.*" Perhaps it came when we faced some decision. Sometimes even in listening and talking, she would direct our thoughts to new heights and new dreams . . . and a new path through life was opened. We found ourselves looking at a new horizon.

To some or all of us she gave the "*Daisy of Love and Compassion.*" The kind word spoken. The good deed she did for us when we thought no one was noticing us or cared for us. The joy she found in doing for others also caught our attention. And we rejoiced, for she showed us what God meant when he said we should care for our neighbor.

But most important of all, she shared with us the "*Daisy of Faith.*" And for that we are the more richly blessed! For you see, she showed us that whatever else could be said of life — it was beautiful — for beyond us was God who cared so much for us that he gave his Son that we all might have Life, and that, more abundantly. For did she not encourage us (and even show us), once, twice, yea many times, to come and see what the Lord had done? In nature there is God's beauty; look at the daisy. In life there is God's love, for God is the Resurrection and the Life. She reminded us that nothing would ever be able to separate us from this love of God, found in Jesus Christ, our Lord. Not any sickness. Nor pain. Nor things present — like suffering from cancer. Nor things to come, like heartache and sorrow. All the treatments and pain which afflicted mind and body would bear witness to the fact that we carry in our "mortal bodies the death of Jesus, so that his life may also be seen in our bodies," (2 Corinthians 4:10) and our suffering be glory to God. Nothing would separate us from God . . . *nothing!* We had and will continue to have Life in Christ! Forever! You, too, come and see what the Lord has done!

And we will have missed her witness to us, if we fail, in turn, to give to others this same "daisy-a-day"

. . . the daisies of laughter, wisdom and hope, love and faith. So in your life, share with others this "daisy-a-day" that Bus has in her lifetime so richly given to us!

Now, may God's peace be ours. This day. Always. Amen.

Hope!

A. Donald Main

SETTING: *This meditation was delivered during a church funeral for the wife of the church council president. She was an outstanding member. Her death was a painful ordeal as she suffered from bone cancer.*

TEXTS: *John 14:1-6*
Revelation 7:9-17

Hope!

Hope . . . there are a variety of hopes and dreams in life. Think back for a moment to your childhood years — when life was somewhat carefree, when your cares were few in number — there were countless things you hoped to receive. If you were a boy, your hope might have been for a new bicycle on your fifth birthday. Perhaps as a young girl you had hoped for a special new doll. Childhood hopes. So simple. So free. Children with wild hope . . . hope because these children knew that because their parents loved them so very much, those parents would do their very best to fulfill the hopes.

But what do we hope for when we are face to face with death? Is there hope? Is hope possible?

Yes, indeed! Hope is possible!

Christians call it the "hope of the righteous." Our Christian hope is not a wild dream that if we want it badly enough, then our heavenly Father will grant it. Rather, our Christian hope is a firm confidence that what God has promised to us, his earthly children, he will give.

Yet we find it hard to possess hope as we gather today in this church and worship God during this funeral service for Millie. Each and every one of us has lost a beautiful part of our lives, because of what Millie did, as a wife, a mother, a sister, a neighbor, a good friend. We long for her "wonderful way" of living life . . . a way which spoke ever so deeply and meaningfully of the love of God flowing from her to others. As a member of the congregation noted, "She was always there — her steadfastness, her faithfulness, her smile." There is a sting to death that is not removed while on this side of eternity. So, for us today, we hold the Christian hope of the righteous high before us!

That hope is a special word God has for the dying, those who grieve, and for those who are broken-hearted. That word is: EASTER. To you who are now so troubled, our Lord Jesus says, "Let not your hearts be troubled. You believe in God, believe also in me. In my Father's house are many mansions; if it were not so, I would have told you. I go to prepare a place for you." (John 14:1-2)

That is the Easter promise. "Even though you die, yet shall you live."

This is God's promise to you and to me. But then, our Lord also says, "Lo, I am with you always." That, too, is God's eternal promise to you, to me.

What that promise means is given more clarity as Jesus speaks about his Father's house. He indicates it has many large rooms or areas, and that he himself has gone to make this ready for the believer. And then, John, in the book of Revelation, gives even more detail to our picture. He does not tell us about bloodless, stained-glass window Christian figures. John speaks about simple and ordinary Christian men and women, like you, like me, like Millie, who, in their earthly life, sought to be like Christ. Perhaps they were slaves or school teachers, plumbers or salesmen, housewives, mothers, farmers, railroaders — all of whom, because they were witnesses of Christ's Resurrection, followed their Lord in thought, word, and deed.

And what is their reward? Language is a poor instrument to describe heavenly life, but John does his best. And the result is a beautiful picture in language which comes simply to this: "Now at last they are able to serve God day and night. Their tears of frustration, their weariness of mind and body, their hurts, their pain, the illnesses, the suffering — all these earthly woes are gone. The Lamb in the midst of the throne will be their shepherd, and he will guide them to springs of living water. And God will wipe away every tear from their eyes."

That is our Christian hope. A hope that we, who have faith in the Risen Lord Jesus, the Christ, will indeed share in eternal life.

Take that hope seriously. Share that hope in word and deed. Amen.

A Gift For A Friend

Stanley C. Sneeringer

SETTING: *This sermon was delivered in the funeral home for a long-time member of the church who had died following a lengthy illness.*

TEXT: *Ephesians 2:1-10*

Jamie Thomas knew he was going to die. He was a leukemia victim who had known for three months that he did not have long to live. One Saturday, he watched his family build a snowman in a rare autumn Texas snowstorm. That night he died. Jamie was five years old.

Jamie's parents had tried to buoy up his spirits by talking to him about God and about Heaven as a place without pain, without hurt. They told him Heaven was where Ronnie lived. Ronnie, another leukemia victim with whom Jamie had become good friends, had died while both were in the hospital. Saddened about his friend's death, Jamie wanted to give Ronnie a present — a stuffed animal named "Tiger." "When I go to heaven," Jamie told everyone, "I want to bring 'Tiger' to my friend."

It seems easy to accept death as natural as we sit here today. We are confronted by a coffin and a body and we know that we too will be here someday. Should we accept death as the way things were meant to be? I cannot. Based on what I know of God in Jesus Christ, we were not meant to die; we were not meant to suffer pain, illness, rejection, hatred, hurt, or loneliness. These and all the other sins were not part of God's original intention of creation. God created the heavens and the earth, and he saw that it was good. Never did he intend death to be humanity's end. Jesus, too, saw death as the direct opposite to God's will. It is we rebellious sinners who have made death what it is — the final denial of God's plan for the world he created. We have made it the end of life.

But, that's the rub. God is God, and his intentions will not be subverted. His plan of union with him is still his desire. He fully intends to disavow death's apparent naturalness, no matter what the form. "God's mercy is so splendid, and his love for us is so great, that while we were spiritually dead in our disobedience, he brought us to life with Christ." (Ephesians 2) What is natural is life. What is natural is love. What is natural is salvation. What is natural is an open-ended future.

That is the gospel — the gracious but firm "No" by God to apparent naturalness of sin and death. Jamie's parents pointed to this open-ended future. So did Jamie Thomas when he wanted to bring his friend a gift.

We all know and share in our hearts the gifts that Harry Shover had given to us. Each one of us has received something from this man over the years. Probably the greatest gift that I received from him was the gift of his skills as a cartoonist when he helped Walt Disney put together "Snow White and the Seven Dwarfs." This gift, which is still being shared by millions of young and old alike, is the gift that Harry Shover has given to me. Each one of us here today has received his or her own gifts from Harry.

And now, Harry has received a gift. It is the same gift that God has given us — the gift of his Son, Jesus Christ. "It is by God's grace that you have been saved . . . He did this to demonstrate for all time to come, the extraordinary greatness of his grace in the love he showed us in Christ Jesus." (Ephesians 2:5b-6) God has given us the gift of sainthood through Christ. By his death and resurrection he has given us the hope that, in the coming years, he will continue to show his immeasurable grace through an open-ended future that looks beyond the apparent naturalness of the grave.

For Harry, that has come to mean that he is now with the God and Father of us all. He is part of the full intention of God's plan for humanity — eternal life. He has inherited in full the gift which we, here, have only partially received.

For us here today that means living this day and every day as a part of a glorious plan for a beautiful future. It is a future, shaped by God, toward which we can live confidently. It is a future which faith and hope opens to us as life. It is a future with purpose — to preach and be the body of Christ.

We have work to do. As Christians we are buoyed by his gift of grace. We are buoyed by the open-ended future that God's gift of Jesus Christ gives to us. We are buoyed by the life of faith and hope that sees us through death. We are buoyed by the ability to serve our fellow human beings in a life of freedom and joy. "For it is by God's grace that you have been saved by faith. It is not a result of your own efforts, but God's gift so that no one can boast about it. God has made us what we are, and in our union with Christ Jesus he has created us for a life of good deeds which he has already prepared for us to do." (Ephesians 2:8-10)

May Harry Shover's gift be yours — a gift of grace for a life of good deeds, through Christ our Lord. Amen.

STORIES OF

SNOW-CROWNED AGE

We Praise God's Holy Name

Dr. Donald R. Heiges

SETTING: *This homily was delivered at the funeral of Abdel Ross Wentz. The Service was conducted on July 22, 1976, in the Chapel of the Abiding Presence on the campus of the Lutheran Theological Seminary, Gettysburg, Pennsylvania, where Dr. Wentz had been president.*

We are met here this morning in a service of thanksgiving for the life and work of Christ's faithful servant, Abdel Ross Wentz. We are met here to praise God for the gift of this remarkable man who, for almost threescore years and ten, gave himself in service to this community, to Gettysburg College, to Gettysburg Seminary, to the Lutheran Church in this country and throughout the world, and to the ecumenical movement. Members of his family and of his wide circle of friends will mourn because of the pain of separation, and for this pain we seek divine comfort and healing; but this is primarily a time of rejoicing that God saw fit to make us the beneficiaries of the life and work of Abdel Ross Wentz.

Since many of us were privileged to know him face to face, we tended to forget that here was a man of worldwide renown who played a major role in shaping not only the Lutheran Church in this country and the National Council of Churches, but also the Lutheran World Federation and the World Council of Churches.

This renown was concretely evidenced at the Testimonial Dinner on October 3, 1951, in recognition of his retirement from the presidency of this Seminary, when no fewer than sixteen persons presented tributes on behalf of the many national and international bodies in which he was a familiar and honored figure, while many bishops and church presidents, along with ordinary pastors and lay people, who could not be at the dinner, paid their tributes in letters filled with superlatives.

Next to his devoted wife and family, the object of his love and labors was, of course, the Lutheran Theological Seminary at Gettysburg. On the occasion of his nintieth birthday I wrote to him:

Of all the sons of the School of Prophets set upon the glorious Hill in Gettysburg, you are, in my judgment, the greatest! Your only competitor for this honor is Samuel Simon Schmucker, our founder. It has been you, during your decades of service, who has made the most impressive, permanent contributions to the life of the Seminary, as well as the most impressive contributions to the life of the Church at large.

As teacher and scholar and administrator and wise counselor, you shaped the lives and destinies of hundreds and hundreds of students in preparation for the ministry of the Church. As planner and builder, you changed the face of the whole campus, and made Gettysburg one of the most beautiful seminaries in the country. As author and editor and translator you have influenced thousands of clerical and lay members of the Church far beyond the family of the Seminary.

In short, the debt of this school of theology to you is monumental. The Abdel Ross Wentz Library will be a perpetual reminder to students now and to generations of students to come of the great man whose name the building bears. It will remind us of the incalculable debt the Seminary will always owe to Abdel Ross Wentz.

His first love, however, was his family, and the role he enjoyed most was that of husband and father and grandfather. He was proud of the family and their accomplishments. He rejoiced with them in their joys, and shared with them in their sorrows. He, along with you, has known the heights of happiness as well as the depths of grief. He always seemed, to me, to be the epitome of "the family man," and because he was, his loved ones will miss him very much.

As we share this loss together, I invite you to join me in praising God, the Holy One, who created Abdel Ross Wentz.

* For the depth and dynamic of his faith in God our Father, in Christ our Lord and Saviour, and in the Holy Spirit, our guide and comforter;
* For the power of his preaching the Word, for the joy of his shepherding God's people, for the persistence of his dedication to what he believed to be true and right;
* For the clarity, the vigor, and the authority of his teaching which helped immeasurably to equip many generations of seminarians for the Church's ministry;

We Praise God's Holy Name.

* For the thoroughness of his scholarship and the excitement of his diction that gained him recognition as one of Lutheranism's most respected historians;
* For the substantial contribution he made to the preparation of the Revised Standard Version of the Bible (for the increase in understanding of God's Word in this age);
* For the wisdom and boundless energy of his administration of the Seminary which saw new curricula fashioned, the faculty strengthened, a campus transformed in beauty and usefulness;

We Praise God's Holy Name.

* For his role in the founding of the American Association of Theological Schools and his strong support of high academic and ethical standards in the field of seminary education;
* For his enduring commitment to, and service in, the cause of bringing the Gosepl to all nations through the worldwide mission of the Church;
* For his pioneering leadership in movements leading to the formation of the Lutheran World Federation and the World Council of Churches, and to increasing significant Lutheran and ecumenical cooperation in this land;

We Praise God's Holy Name.

For these and many other blessings which have come to us through this man's long and noble life, we stand in awe and gratitude, and pray God to enable us, members of the Church Militant, to pursue in our own ways the high goals to which he gave himself.

Glory be to the Father, and to the Son, and to the Holy Spirit: As it was in the beginning, is now, and ever shall be. Amen.

Wisdom Is With The Aged

S. Cyril Hurnyak

SETTING: *This meditation was preached at the funeral of an elderly church member who died three months after her husband's death.*

TEXTS: O God, from my youth thou hast taught me,
and I still proclaim thy wondrous deeds.
So even to old age and gray hairs,
O God, do not forsake me,
till I proclaim thy might
to all generations to come.
Thy power and thy righteousness,
O God, reach the high heavens.
[Psalms 71:17-19]

Wisdom is with the aged,
and understanding in length of days.
[Job 12:12]

My ministry has been brief. Yet, in this short span of time, I have discovered how rewarding are the common, ordinary moments of life. Great are the things of everyday. Rich are the blessings that emerge by sharing life with the humble, everyday folks we meet and greet.

One such blessing was created by the lives of two humble people: Ray and Margret Maute. From them I received a reward: I saw the extreme beauty which shines out in the lives of folks who are devoted and very much in love. But you know what I mean, because you observed it, too.

Ray and Margret — two people, romanically in love, even in the twilight of their years. The afflictions which haunt old age could not end their childlike devotion . . . their concern for one another.

Their example brought to mind the devotion of yet another couple described in a poem written by the late 18th Century Scottish laureate, Robert Burns. In his poem, "John Anderson, My Jo," he poetically recounts the youthful love of a Scottish lad and lassie. They frolicked on the hill . . . the same hill on which they would rest together in death.

John Anderson my jo, John,
 When we were first Acquent,
Your locks were like the raven,
 Your bonnie brow was brent;
But now your brow is beld, John,
 Your locks are like the snaw,
But blessings on your frosty pow [head],
 John Anderson my jo!

John Anderson my jo, John,
 We clamb the hill thegither,
And monie a cantie day, John,
 We've had wi' ane anither:
Now we maun totter down, John,
 And hand in hand we'll go,
And sleep thegither at the foot,
 John Anderson my jo!

Resting together. That now is the gift of Ray and Margret. Three months ago Ray came to life's end. Now Margret joins her love. They, too, now rest on the hill together.

Yet, before this rest, Margret revealed her own poetic notion: "the loneliness is still there. I still feel the pain of separation from Ray." But in spite of these strong feelings, she demonstrated an ability to bear suffering, and she did it graciously.

Yes, the cross of suffering was a real part of Margret's life. It was a real part of Ray's life. It was a real part of their life together. Ray's coronary condition and Margret's crippling arthritis made suffering literally a "household word." But did you notice something important, something that shows "wisdom is with the aged?" I did. I noticed their determination was an inspiration to many. I noticed that their afflictions served to strengthen their love and devotion, their compassion and concern. "They were afflicted in every way, but not crushed." They were a "living" witness to our Lenten theme: Love Suffers.

And the foundation of this "suffering love" was the Word of God. They knew our Father's love was so great that he gave up his Son, in order that we might have eternal life. They witnessed to a living God who blesses the common and ordinary people of life. They acknowledged that, because of God, we may be made new, and be fulfilled in the potential God holds for each of us who believes. Their example demonstrated that the cross is not an inward journey; it is an outward one. The cross causes us all to reach out beyond ourselves and behold another. Indeed, their faith was humbling to see and experience. Indeed, their faith was a rare and beautiful thing to behold!

This day, let us learn from their example:

* Let us learn that their commitment to each other was not just instinct, it was nurtured by unconditional love.

* Let us learn that each day we must accept one another.

* Let us learn that love is not self-serving, it is given in service to one another.

* Let us learn that, we, too, along with the Psalmist, Ray, and Margret, "must still proclaim" God's "wondrous deeds."

I have learned from Ray and Margret. Have you learned, too? Have you seen, as I have, that "wisdom is with the aged?" If so, then you are richly blessed. And with such wisdom and faith, we, too, can walk, like Margret and Ray, in the light of our resurrected Lord. And may we all come to that day when we rejoice in the "power and righteousness which reach beyond the heavens," for now that is where Margret and Ray continue in their love with the eternal presence of our loving Heavenly Father.

The Teacher

Hobert B. Johnson

SETTING: *This meditation was preached at the memorial service for an elderly woman who was an outstanding public school teacher.*

TEXTS: *Jesus said to her, "I am the resurrection and the life; he who believes in me, though he die, yet shall he live, and whoever lives and believes in me shall never die."* [John 11:25-26]

Because I live, you will live also. [John 14:19]

When a loved one dies, we experience an emotional turmoil of heart-rending grief. It is shocking, painful, even physically exhausting. This is both understandable and normal . . . not something from which we need to flee, nor feel embarrassment. In fact, it is in a very real sense an expression of love . . . love that must be acknowledged and expressed, whether by joy or by grief. "If you love deeply, you will grieve deeply." Thus it follows that the "choice to love . . . in its most mature dimension . . . is also the courage to grieve."

Washington Irving described the beautiful relationship of love and grief this way: "There is a sacredness in tears. They are not the mark of weakness, but of power. They speak more eloquently than ten thousand tongues. They are messengers of overwhelming grief . . . and of unspeakable love."

Martha Edith Chambers, the teacher, was not a hard person to love. As a daughter and sister, she was loyal and devoted . . . of whom it was so natural and proper to be proud. As a wife . . . faithful and considerate . . . making strong the bond of mutual love and respect. As a mother, Edith was understanding, concerned and trusting . . . making mature, stable, and responsible adults the norm for her son and daughter. As a friend, Edith was considerate and quietly diligent. Yes, in all our encounters with Edith, she taught us much; she inevitably raised the sights of all of us by her unpretentious but effective example.

And as a public school teacher, Edith Chambers was, and is, the epitome of a great profession. At the age of six, she said she decided she would be a teacher. And teach she did . . . in Illinois, in Brady Lake, and in Kent. Teaching, we are told, is essentially a twofold task: 1) to impart knowledge or skills; to give instruction; and 2) to show, to point out, to direct, to guide and lead. Edith fulfilled both of these roles in a peerless fashion by supplementing her training, skills, and experience with a warm, genuine personality. Her example of deep love and respect and personal concern for each of her students was apparent to all who were fortunate enough to know her, and call her by the name of "teacher."

We thank God for having known her . . . for having shared life with a true teacher. We do not curse him for losing her. For she is not lost; we believe her to be with him. She is not lost to us as much as she is loosed among us. The pattern of life which she discovered belongs to all of us as a beacon light. She found her life's meaning and joy by investing it in others. When I spoke with Edith about the love and the work and the promises and the hope we have in Christ, she acknowledged her faith and convictions by a squeeze of the hand and a blink of her eyes. She was a beautiful person. I believe, with you, she is now a beautiful immortal being. Why? Because all she did was so deeply rooted in the Master Teacher.

In closing, I would like to explain the basis for such a belief by reading a brief excerpt from Peter Marshall's classic sermon, "The Grave in the Garden."*

The words are these:

"A great realization dawns over you, you hear His
    voice:
'Lo, I am with you always, even unto the end of the
    world.'
'Whosoever believeth in me, though he were dead, yet
    shall he live, and whosoever believeth in me,
        shall never die . . .'
'Because I live, ye shall live also.'

Because we can't stand it any longer — in the secret
places of our hearts, we cry out to God for help — and
then it comes, the supreme miracle for which we have
been seeking.

It is so tremendous a thing that we can't describe it.

It is so delicate a thing that we can't even bring it into
view for anybody else to look at.

We can never explain it to anybody else.
We know only that it is true.

The Voice has said: 'Because I live, ye shall live also.'

Our hearts knew all along it must be so. It was what we
wanted to hear, and now that we have heard it, we feel
that we have solved the mystery of life.

'If a man die, shall he live again?'
Yes, because the Resurrection is a fact.
Aye, and I, too, shall live, because I know it's true."

*"The Grave in the Garden" from Mr. Jones, Meet the Master:
Sermons and Prayers of Peter Marshall. Copyright © 1949, 50 by
Fleming H. Revell Company.

In Sight Of Salvation

John P. Seltzer

SETTING: *This sermon was preached at the funeral of a woman who died at the age of 87, only two months after she was baptized. Although she worshiped at any number of churches during her lifetime, she never became a church member until her baptism. Consequently, she was quite unknown to the preacher. She had nine children, thirty-five grandchildren, and fifty-five great-grandchildren, most of whom attended the service.*

TEXT: *Luke 2:22-35*

Simeon was a good Jew. He had lived a long life. He had seen much. He had heard much. Moreover, he was a righteous man because he obeyed the Law of Moses. And because of that obedience, he was respected and loved by the people around him — his friends, his family. He was, indeed, a man of stature. And it was to this man that God made a very personal promise: before Simeon died, he would be permitted to see the promised Messiah . . . something that every good Jew dreams and hopes for all his life. This promise was made to Simeon by God himself. Small wonder, then, that Simeon was determined to live until the special time had come for the ceremony of purification. And as it happened, Mary and Joseph took Jesus to the Temple on the eighth day after his birth. They did this to fulfill Jewish Law. And the Spirit of God moved Simeon so that he recognized Jesus as the promised Christ. He picked Jesus up in his arms, looked at Mary, and blessed God, saying, "You finally fulfilled your promise, Lord. Now, Lord, you can take me in your peace as you have promised." There is little more that we know of Simeon. We do not know what he did. We do not know where he came from, what he liked, what he disliked. What we do know is that God fulfilled his promise before Simeon's death. So, Simeon was fully assured that the salvation of mankind had come in Jesus of Nazareth.

When I think of Edith Hanson, I am reminded of Simeon because I personally did not know Edith very well. As a matter of fact, I don't know what she liked or disliked in life. I do not know what occupied most of her time, except for the fact she must have spent a lot of time raising her children. You, her family and friends, are a testament to that great deed of love that she accomplished. Even so, during my visits in the hospital, she was not physically able to talk with me. So, as with Simeon, I do not know very much about Edith.

You folks, her friends and family, know so much more than I do. You are the ones who really have the story of her life in your hearts and minds today — what you are feeling, what you are thinking, the memories. You are the ones who are called to share those thoughts and feelings, and I encourage you to do that . . . to share with each other, to build each other up, and in so doing, to give thanks to God for Edith's life, through which you have been blessed.

What I can say is this: Edith was a devout and upright woman; and like Simeon, Edith came to know her Lord Jesus Christ in a special way, only a few months before her death — at her Baptism. That was a very special moment for her. It was a special moment for you as well.

Because of that Baptism and her faith, what we can proclaim today is the fact that she was blessed with the fullest assurance of eternal life that is given to each and every one of us. Sure, it is important that Jesus suffered and died for us on the cross. It is, however, the event of Resurrection that makes the hope for eternal life something that is so glorious and so filled with joy, that even in the midst of our grief today, we can say, "It is time to celebrate and rejoice!" Edith knew fully that God loved her and continues to love her . . . that was the greatest comfort she could possibly possess. That is the greatest comfort you and I can possess. God does not abandon us. As Paul says, "Nothing can separate us from the love of Christ . . . not even death." It is through the resurrection that, indeed, the promise of eternal life is real, not only for Edith now, but for you and me, for all time. No longer does she have to put up with the pain of sickness; no longer does she have to have fear in her heart. Those things are passed for Edith. Now she has the glorious life that has no end.

That is the *Good News!* And it does seem strange to talk about good news at a funeral — but that's what is important for us to remember. Today we must hold close to our hearts the Good News of eternal life, and let the Spirit strengthen our faith. We, too, can know fully what Edith knows completely — the promise of eternal life through Christ Jesus is a gift given to each and every one of us.

May God bless you as he has blessed Edith.

May God strengthen you and lift you up with his Spirit. Amen.

On Making The Great Crossing

Robert W. Stackel

SETTING: *This sermon was preached at the funeral of a woman who came to the United States as a young woman from Sweden. She died at the age of 82.*

TEXT: *On that day, when evening had come, he said to them, "Let us go across to the other side."* [*Mark 4:35*]

When Olga was a young lady of 22, she made the great crossing from Sweden, her homeland, to the United States, her adopted land. When she was an older lady of 82, she made the great crossing from this life to her true homeland in heaven.

The day when evening came for Olga was last Friday. The thing to remember is that evening comes to every life. For some, it comes early; for some, it comes late. But evening always comes. A girl who married a serviceman in Fairbanks, Alaska, wrote, "What I can't get used to is evening falling about two o'clock in the afternoon in a land where daylight is only a few hours a day." For some, evening comes that early in life.

For Olga, evening came late. She lived a long life. God gave her to us for over eighty years. But she was ready for evening. Her membership in her congregation went back forty years. She was a woman of faith and prayer. Her trust was in her Savior. There is no substitute for careful, lifelong, spiritual preparation against the time when evening falls, whether early or late. As God's ambassador, I plead with you: prepare now for the evening time of life. When the moment of the great crossing comes, it is too late to prepare.

Hear again the words of our Lord: "On that day, when evening had come, he said to them, 'Let us go across to the other side.' " Those who trust in Christ never have to make the great crossing alone. "Let us go across to the other side," Jesus said. At another time our Lord promised, "When I go and prepare a place for you, I will come again and will take you to myself, that where I am you may be also." When Olga was a young lady, she did not make the great crossing of the Atlantic Ocean alone. Others were with her on the boat. Last Friday she did not have to make the great crossing alone either. Jesus, true to his promise, came to take her across. What a comfort it is to us today that Christ came to escort her personally to the Father! When the burden of the flesh had become intolerable on this side, as God knew best of all, then Christ came to take her to the other side, where all is new and fresh again.

When Jesus crossed the sea with his disciples that night, it was not very far across. It did not take very long. When Olga made the great crossing last Friday with Jesus, it was not even that far and it did not take even that long. Christ promised the thief on the cross, "Today you will be with me in Paradise." That near and that swift is the mercy of God to guide the faithful to eternal life in Christ.

There is a word inside that word "across" that makes possible for us the great crossing to our Father's home. That word is, "cross," the cross of Christ. His great loving sacrifice on Calvary's cross had Olga in mind, even as he had all of us in mind. His Resurrection had Olga in mind, as well as all of us. Our crossing is possible because of his cross for us.

On the day that Olga died, the beautiful Amaryllis flower, that a friend had given her weeks before, burst open its first showy red blossom . . . a giant display of dazzling red. It was a symbol of the blossoming for her of the flower of everlasting life. Olga, the seamstress, who made clothes for other people, can now be fitted in the garments of righteousness made for her by our Savior's death and Resurrection for us all . . . and she can walk in white before the Lord.

Last Friday, the greatest crossing for Olga can best be summed up in the words of the Bible, "On that day, when evening had come, (Jesus) said to them, 'Let us go across to the other side.' "

Rooted In Christ

King Wynkoop

SETTING: *This sermon was preached at the funeral of an elderly woman who was confirmed shortly before her death.*

TEXT: *Psalms 23*
Romans 8:37-39

Families are a beautiful part of God's creation. It is good for family members to spend time together. It is good for families to come together. Families share precious memories. In a family, one can reflect on events, or on what this or that family member did or said. During such moments, you begin to learn to know each other; you begin to discover the other member's unique and individual traits, habits, loves, interests, and characteristics. Along with this discovery of a person's life, there are often surprises. Sometimes humorous things pop up. And what makes this family sharing of special interest is the surprise of finding what trait or characteristic, or likeness, you may have inherited or learned from a parent or grandparent. You trace your roots. You uncover your origins. You unveil the many strong ties of love that knit you together as members of a growing family . . . how you are a part of each other's life.

Yes, it is good to do this, because often we like to think that our generation has sprung up without any roots in past foundations. We imagine all that is good comes without any contribution from other generations.

Through the family of the church, I have come to know Laura. Among the many notes in the melody of her life, I heard and admired the note of "thankfulness" the most. Laura's life was rooted in thankfulness. She was most thankful for:

* her son and his family, and their seven children;

* the many years of health, though there was also sickness;

* her garden, and the sun and rain which nourished the seeds to green and harvest;

* the reality that she could help her son earn a doctorate, even though she had only a fourth grade education; the job as a waitress . . . the job which gave her tips (never more than $1600 a year) which helped put her son through school;

* a son who worked hard to become a professor;

* the gift of life.

As we now offer our note of thanks to God for Laura Epley . . . as we honor her memory . . . I would like to share a story about some special experiences of recent months. The story reveals how Laura discovered her roots in Christ. You might call the experiences I am about to describe a new direction, a turning to God, a coming home. But listen to my story.

It all started when a neighbor, Verna Klingler, began visiting Laura. You see, Verna's home is not far from Laura's home. So it was natural for her to stop by to visit. Sometimes Verna would mention she had been to worship or to a Bible study. Occasionally she spoke about her friends at church. Quite often she spoke about what Christ and the church means to her. (Incidentally, Verna is attending this church funeral today.)

Then, Laura took three important steps in her life. She made three decisions. First, she told Verna, "I want a minister to visit. I need to talk." The senior pastor called on her. He brought flowers. He talked. They prayed. On the first and later visits, the conversation centered on Christ.

Then, second, Laura decided to become a member of Emmanuel Church. Following a period of instruction, she was received into the Christian fellowship by the rite of confirmation. She heard the pastor's questions: "Do you believe in God the Father, God the Son, and God the Holy Spirit?" "Do you promise to abide in this faith?" Her response: "Yes, by the help of God."

Laura's third decision was to receive Holy Communion. I visited her, and we communed together in her living room. She heard the words of forgiveness . . . she received the bread and the wine . . . she heard the benediction: "May the Body of our Lord Jesus Christ and his precious Blood strengthen and preserve you unto eternal life."

Yes, in the closing months of her life, Laura made three key decisions . . . perhaps because she sensed some "unfinished business" . . . perhaps because she wanted to anchor her life more firmly in the Lord.

Knowing her age, and having had extensive sickness, Laura must have known that death was near. She often thought about it. What is the meaning of life and death? How was she meant to prepare for death?

She answered by talking with a pastor, being confirmed, and receiving the assurance of forgiveness in Holy Communion.

Laura could now say and live the words of the Shepherd Psalm: "Even though I walk through the valley of the shadow of death, I will fear no evil, for thou art with me. Thy rod and thy staff, they comfort me."

Laura discovered her roots in Christ!

During seminary, one of the professors told of his visit to a woman in her home. He arrived to find her working on a loom. The article she was working on looked like a 'bunch of odds and ends.' The colors seemed to be mixed and in the wrong places. The pattern didn't make any sense to him. In fact, it looked like a mess, and he told her so. He asked what she was doing. She began to laugh. She revealed that the reason it looked this way was because she was working on the rug upside-down. She turned it right side up, and immediately he saw a beautiful pattern of color and design. It was truly a work of art.

The professor indicated that life is much like this. We are able to see life only from our side. We see the loose ends. Often we fail to see any design or beauty or pattern. When life is filled with 'ups and downs,' suffering and sickness, it is difficult to discover any purpose or design.

But if we could see life from God's vantage point, it would be different. We would see God working, creating, and making all things new. Then life would take on an entirely new meaning.

When we look at death from God's vantage point, we can also get a clearer vision.

* We picture death as coming to destroy; let us rather picture Christ coming to save.

* We think of death as ending; let us rather think of life as beginning, and that more abundantly.

* We think of a loss; let us think of the gains.

* We think of going away; let us think of arriving.

For you see, the roots, the faith in Christ that Laura discovered . . . and the faith we have allows us, as Christians, to sing with Paul:

In all these things we are more than conquerors through him who loved us . . . I am sure that nothing can separate us from the love of God in Christ.

It is this good news that Laura discovered during the final months of life. It is this good news which enabled Laura to commit her life to Christ. And in her quiet way, she made her witness to Christ, the Lord of Life and Death. She had discovered the "roots" of real living.

What about us, the living? Can we sing with the psalmist, "surely goodness and mercy shall follow me all the days of my life?" What is our relationship to the Lord of Life? Have we been found by God?

Some liken faith to raising the sail of our little boat until it becomes caught up in the soft winds above and picks up speed . . . not from anything within itself, but from the endless resources of God.

Are your sails open and receptive to all God would share with you?

Are you ready to discover your roots in Christ? Only you can answer!

STORIES OF

PERSONS STRICKEN

SUDDENLY

God's Intention

George W. Gaiser

SETTING: *This sermon was preached at the funeral of a man, aged forty-one, who died of a cerebral hemorrhage. It was preached by a guest pastor in the home church of which the deceased was very much a part.*

TEXT: *Lamentations 3:24-33*

We are gathered for a memorial service for Eldon Prince. None of us is here because he or she wants to be. If we had our way we would be at home or at our jobs or in school. But we have not had our way. Death has intruded into a family, friendships, a congregation, and a community. That means change for each of those groups because Eldon was a staunch participant in each, and Eldon is dead. That is why we are here.

Specifically, I am here because the family asked me to be, and this congregation and its' pastor assented. I am supposed to answer the unanswerable question, make the horribly wrong right, iron smooth all the wrinkles.

Well, I can't do that. I take comfort in the fact that one much better and more equipped than I couldn't either. In the story from which Rev. Ruch read the Gospel (the raising of Lazarus), Jesus, who had the answer all of us here would like, nevertheless had problems. It wasn't all that easy. "Jesus wept."

So we all weep, and weep we should. What would it say about the quality of Eldon's relationship with us if we did not? But weeping is only part of it. If Eldon's death means only weeping, we shall be the poorer for his life. In an effort to get beyond weeping, recognizing fully that the questions will not all be answered, let me read a section from Lamentations, chapter three:

The Lord, I say, is all that I have;
therefore I will wait for him patiently.
The Lord is good to those who look for him, to all
who seek him;
it is good to wait in patience and sigh for
deliverance by the Lord.
It is good, too, for a man to carry the yoke in his
youth.
Let him sit alone and sigh if it is heavy upon him;
let him lay his face in the dust and there may yet be
hope.
Let him turn his cheek to the smiter
and endure full measure of abuse;
for the Lord will not cast off
his servants for ever.
He may punish cruelly, yet he will have compassion
in the fullness of his love;
he does not willingly afflict
or punish any mortal man.

The clincher in that section is the last line, "he does not willingly afflict or punish any mortal man." The implication is clear. God intends to make something even out of affliction!

But what can he make out of the death of one so young? In answer to that, I point to something one of Eldon's daughters said to me a day or so ago. She told me that her father had accomplished what he wanted to accomplish in life. Hers was a mature argument for quality life. I do not want Eldon to be dead either, but it helps to recall that while he was among us, his was a quality approach to life. It may even help further to compare his approach to his life to the life of his Lord (and ours) at the one point of the youth of each. As Christians, we are ill-equipped to argue for quantity when we base all that we are or ever shall be on the life of one who died at age thirty-three.

Another thing I think we can make out of Eldon's death is forgiveness. That is significant, since there is probably no one here without guilt. Somewhere in each of us is that voice which says, "If only I had," or "If only I had not" while Eldon was still alive.

I talked with his family about that, too. I tried to get at his nature with them. His girls came through like champs. They remembered that even in his anger, there was still love, that the relationship of family members with him was dependent upon his love for them, not what they had or had not done.

I submit that Eldon was a good teacher in that. The 130th Psalm says it well: "If thou Lord shouldst mark iniquities, O Lord, who shall stand?" The answer to that question is nobody. That is what J. S. Bach is talking about in the *St. Matthew Passion* where he writes, "When I depart from Thee, depart Thou not from me." God's relationship with us, with Eldon, his wife, his daughters, mother and sister, friends, church, preachers, and community is based on his love for us all, not on our response. That is cause for great rejoicing, even at the same time as it is an invitation to use Eldon's life as an argument for forgiveness. Pastor Johnson will lead us soon in the Lord's Prayer. Jesus reminds us in it that as we forgive, so are we forgiven, and the other way around. And if we can learn forgiveness here, then I also submit that Eldon will not have died in vain.

Let me conclude by suggesting that this be a beginning. Let me suggest further that each of you is involved in the rest of the story, for the rest of the story is your lives and the way in which you talk together about what Eldon has been for you. Keep that Eldon alive. Talk about him even when that seems painful. The other way, to be silent, is ultimately more painful, for it makes it appear as if his life were insignificant and unnoticed. Again, we have an excellent teacher in that one who died on a cross nearly 2,000 years ago.

Christians operate on the notion that by keeping alive his live and death, somehow new life will be brought into existence right now. Out of the grievous affliction of Good Friday comes the glory of Easter. Resurrection is a fact not only for Jesus, not only for Eldon, resurrection is a fact for everyone here!

The peace of God which passes all human understanding,

Keep your hearts and your minds in Christ Jesus our Lord. Amen.

For Everything There Is A Season

Herbert S. Garnes, III

SETTING: *This meditation was preached at the funeral of a man, aged sixty-three, who died of a heart attack. He was a faithful church member who served as a Sunday School teacher and church treasurer for over twenty years; he also served on numerous committees of the synod. He was a personal friend and a man who loved gardening.*

TEXT: *Ecclesiastes 3:1-10*

> For everything there is a season:
> a time to be born, and a time to die,
> a time to plant, and a time to pluck up what is
>   planted,
> a time to weep, and a time for joy,
> a time to mourn, and a time for gladness . . .

Ivan Bishop understood the times and seasons of the year. He knew the time to start begonias so they would be in full leaf to put out in the warmth of early summer. He knew the time to pick glads so that the bouquet would have the greatest and longest-lasting beauty. His garden had flowers for all the seasons — tulips for spring, roses for summer, marigolds for fall.

To the novice in the "world of flowers," he was a great help. He could explain why the plant did not bloom at the time the book said that it should, or why the blooms did not last as long as in previous years. He understood that many things affect how long a flower stays in bloom — night temperature and daily amounts of sunshine and moisture. He knew that each flower had its time and purpose, so he planted his garden so that as one flower's blooms were ending, another's were beginning. So, too, the Lord has filled the earth with people who bloom with his love in every generation, and Ivan was one of those blooms.

As we do with flowers, we ask why the lives of some are long and others, like Ivan's, seemingly short. We do not know, but the words of our Gospel tell us that whoever hears the words of Jesus, and believes, has already passed from death to life. Ivan, like the tulips of spring, awaits the resurrection day when all the faithful will bloom in full glory before the Father.

Ivan knew more than flowers and vegetables. He knew people. He said they were his hobby — watching them, that is. But I suspect they were his life. The last few months had been hard for him — he could not be among people as he liked. Ivan knew the times and seasons of those around him. There were the cards, notes, calls, flowers, and vegetables which came at special times, like birthdays, anniversaries, illness, or happiness — he shared in the lives of those around him. For you, Allan, Linda, and Brian, he was a loving and concerned father. For me, a young man just graduated from seminary, he was a friend and a guiding hand. For others, he was a co-worker and leader. Others have been these things too; but, in his life we saw the fruits of God's Holy Spirit in full flower. He was a man of love, joy, peace, patience (Oh, yes, was he patient with me, a young pastor, full of ideas and book learning.), kindness, goodness, faithfulness, gentleness and self-control. As in the parable of the sower, the Word of God that fell at Ivan's heart has brought forth fruit a hundredfold . . . and we have received that fruit.

Because he did touch us in many ways, we have come in our lives to a time of weeping and mourning. It is right and good that we grieve and sorrow. Let us remember, however, that our tears and grief are for our loss and not his. There will never be another person exactly like Ivan in our lives, and nothing can fill the void that his death has created — because of that we mourn, and for that only.

For Ivan, this is a time for joy and gladness. He has heard the call of our Lord, and passed from death to life. The words of Christ from the cross ring clear and true for Ivan: "Truly, truly I say to you, today you will be with me in Paradise." (Luke 23:43) Ivan can experience no greater joy than to rest from his labors and be freed from the sin and death of this world. He trusted in the words of Jesus: "I am the resurrection and the life." (John 11:25) His faith can and should serve as a model for us. This faith and trust in the Lord, and the "acting out" of this faith through the church, was not an isolated part of his life. It was like fertilizer he mixed all through the soil — it gave fresh strength and nourishment to all that came in contact with it . . . and we are much the richer for it.

His work in the church will be missed, but as the flowers of summer replace those of spring, it is now time for others to "come into bloom" in the work of the church. The writer of our lesson from Ecclesiastes asked: "What gain has the worker from his toil?" Ivan knows the answer to that question. It is the kingdom of God. For him the words are true and fitting: "Well done thou good and faithful servant, enter into the joy of my kingdom." (Matthew 25:23)

Ivan knew the times and seasons of life and people. One question remains. Do we know the time and season that is here today? Ivan's seasons have ended, and he has borne much fruit. Can the same be said for you and for me? Jesus has said that every tree that does not bear fruit is cut down and used as fuel for the fire. Let us look at our own lives, for we have been told that now is the acceptable time; today is the day of salvation. Let us commit our lives to our Lord and thereby, being led by the Spirit, we may follow the example that was before us in the life of Ivan Bishop. Then in our last hour we, too, may say in confidence:

O death, where is thy victory?
O death, where is thy sting?
Thanks be to God, who gives us the victory through our Lord Jesus Christ. [1 Corinthians 15:55]

An Appetizer

Carl W. Mangold

SETTING: *This sermon was preached at the church funeral of a sixty-nine year old woman who died following a very severe heart attack, the second in a year. She was always concerned for and about others. A faithful member, she always supported the ministry of the church with her time and talents, prayers and gifts.*

TEXT: *John 11:1-44*

[*The sermon text which follows has been preceded by a brief story of Ann's life and her relationship to pastor and people.*]

You have heard the story of Ann's life. You have recognized, once again, the importance of God in one's life story. Ann would expect me to share just a portion of God's Story, now, with you. So, listen to one chapter of this Story. (The text is read.)

Within this rather extended story is my text for today. It is the shortest verse in the entire Bible: *Jesus wept.* John's Gospel is the only one which relates this story about Jesus' beloved friend, Lazarus. Lazarus had been sick. By the time Jesus arrived, Lazarus had been dead four days. Some Jews are consoling the family.— perhaps in ways much as people have spoken to you and tried to console you these past few days. But, instead of going to the family in order to console them, Jesus went to the tomb. And like you and me . . . he weeps. He weeps because of a friend's death. Jesus, at this moment, also experiences, therefore, the truth of that passage in Ecclesiastes:

*There is a time to be born, and a time to die;
a time to plant, and a time to pluck up what is
    planted;
a time to kill, and a time to heal;
a time to break down, and a time to build up;
a time to weep, and a time to laugh;
a time to mourn, and a time to dance.*

Yes, in this life there is a time for everything. And Jesus, as you and I, wept at the tomb of death. And yet, he knew that in the eternal reaches of God's time, there is something more. For he says to Martha: "I am the resurrection and the life. He who believes in me shall never die."

This he says:

* while Lazarus lies dead;
* only a few chapters before the account of his own death;
* in the midst of his own agony, loss and mourning.

Jesus does not say that the dead will live on in the memories of the living . . . although that may be true in some cases. He indicates something more important: the dead will live on with God through the resurrection, that is, through him. Yet, still, despite his knowledge of God's victory to come in his own resurrection, Jesus weeps. Our text gives us no clearly defined answer as to why Jesus cried. Only one thing is certain: Jesus did not cry because he felt guilty about delaying four days before coming to the aid of an ailing, beloved friend.

This raises the question about Jesus' divine and human natures and their relationship to one another. Here is John's account. We meet the human Jesus of Nazareth crying over the loss of a friend . . . while at the same time he knew the outcome for Lazarus and for himself. Jesus Christ did not feel guilty. But Jesus did weep . . . just as you do now. And because of those tears, our Lord can comfort us because he has been here in grief.

He has gone before us. Now he will walk through the valley of despair . . . loneliness . . . and grief, with us, as our companion on the way. And like the Preacher of Ecclesiastes, we shall find that we will dance again, be healed again, build again, and laugh again . . . as unbelievable as that may now sound. We shall find ourselves laughing with Paul at death and the grave: "O death, where is thy sting? O grave, where is thy victory?" For we know, with Paul, that Christ is the resurrection and the life; Christ has conquered death, and as a result, death has no longer a sting, no longer a victory over us.

True, like Jesus, we weep; but it is for our loss, not for those who have died in the Lord. For those who die in Jesus Christ have God with them.

Yet the sting is there for us. We think it will linger on forever. We find it hard to imagine that we will laugh. So, let me tell you a story. When I was about ten or eleven years old, I was outdoors playing with some friends, the Lipski brothers. Raymond and Mike and I were playing in the front yard when Ray announced that he had just placed his foot over a hole in the ground. Quickly I remembered that this was the very spot where we had seen wasps flying in and out of a hole. Taking charge, I told Ray not to remove his foot, and for Mike to run to the backyard and bring a board so that I could slide it over the hole, while Ray simultaneously slid his foot off of the hole. As I was bending over the spot, with the board in my hand, and my face about six inches from the ground, Ray panicked and removed his foot. Many angry wasps came flying out — directly into my face, stinging me countless times. Needless to say, I left my beloved bicycle where it was and ran home to my parents for comfort. My father soothed my stings. Yet, I must say that at that moment I thought the sting would never go away. But it did. I did eventually stop crying.

In similar fashion, we will reach a point when we cry no more. Jesus likewise reached a point when he ceased to weep. Then he resurrected his beloved friend. He raised him from the tomb. And Jesus' raising of Lazarus is a foretaste, an appetizer of Jesus Christ's own resurrection — and of ours. I know. You know. Ann knew and believed. What? That our redeemer lives! And we know that whoever believes in him, though he or she die, yet shall they live with God. And since our living Redeemer, Jesus Christ, wept and suffered at death's tomb, He can be with you . . . always. Go in peace.

The Inevitable

Richard F. Michael

SETTING: *Preached at the funeral of a middle-aged man who died unexpectedly.*

TEXT: *Romans 8*

The death of our friend, father, husband, and fellow Christian brings the reality of Paul's words to us.
  As he writes, we are sheep led to the slaughter.
    After this, what can be said?
    Death is inevitable.
      It will come to each of us.
      We cannot stop its approach.
We are living, breathing, human beings faced with the unpleasant possibility of non-being . . . of not existing any more.
  The thought shatters our snug, comfortable worlds and confronts us with reality.

  When a loved one dies, death is real.
  Frank's loss is tremendous and the pain almost unbearable.
      Never at any other time have we felt so helpless.
And, yet, we can say to anyone here, faced with what is the hardest, cruelest reality of our lives — here is God.
  He comes, the reality of the resurrection, his resurrection!
And for the Christian, it is not only a time of helplessness, but in being helped.

The Resurrection has been witnessed and attested to by millions of Christians over the 2,000 years since it happened.

Each one who has felt the power and warmth of
Christ's presence
knows that no grave could hold him, or his
ministry.
Here in the fact of death, our friend and our own Christ
comes to claim control, just as he did that first Easter
and so often since.
He comes to proclaim that all things are in his
power, even this.
He comes to assure us that there is no place we can
be separated from him.
No place, that is, unless we choose to build
walls and set up a road block.
No place, except when we choose not to
acknowledge his presence in our lives.
Paul is right as he says . . .
but only if we acknowledge he is here will we feel
his presence.
He gives us his love as a present — what
good is it not opened?
It is times like this, believe it or not, that the road blocks
and walls can go up.
In grief we will feel so sorry for ourselves.
In guilt we will wonder if we could have done
more.
In blame and anger we may even point a finger at
God.
In worry and anxiety we will wonder what we will
do. How we can go on, and we will want to live
in the past, rather than face the future.
But it is also during these times that we can be most
open to his love and presence.
Here we can truly open his gift and begin to
discover the life he has meant for us to have and
to live.
Here we can find, even at his low point in our
fragile, threatened, existence, that even this
cannot separate us from his Love.

And this is what we can say with confidence and hope.
We have his Love!
We are his people!
And nothing, not even death, ours or our loved one's, can separate us from his Love.
Nothing that is but the foolishness of ourselves.
Today as we gather to mourn our loss, we are confronted with that choice between God's power and our foolishness.
As Frank passes from the Church Militant to the Church Triumphant, and gathers us here, it is his final act of ministry for us.
It is Frank who confronts us with his death, and so our death.
But it is Frank's final act of ministry that also reminds us of the power of our God over all things, even this.
As we leave here today, I pray you accept his presence, his Love
for our loved one is now God's and in God's care, for we must go . . . and go on.
Death is the inevitable end of our days.
But how we go on is a choice we make this day with our God.

A Mighty Fortress

Thomas N. Rogers

SETTING: *This meditation was delivered at the funeral of a personal friend, a fifty-one year old man who was born in Greece.*

TEXT: *1 Corinthians 13*

They tell me the reason a safety match is a safety match is because part of the chemicals needed for combustion are in the match, and the rest are in the striking surface of the match book. I compare my encounters with George to the striking of the safety match . . . the coming together of two different chemistries to make light and sometimes heat: the Anglo-Saxon/German and the Greek.

Now we Germans are both blessed and cursed by a narrow view of the world. Blessed because we often enjoy the security of having things neat and buttoned-up. Cursed because security is often boring. We are deprived of mountaintop experiences in life. The Greek, on the other hand, takes a much bigger view of life, but that, too, is a double-edged sword. For the Greek view that lets one exalt on the mountaintop also means one must despair in the valley. And don't we always want what we don't have? I look for the mountaintop and don't want the despair; George looked for the security without the boredom. That is why, perhaps, dissatisfied Germans become neurotics, and Greeks become philosophers and dreamers.

Philosophy is the combination of two Greek words: love and wisdom. A philosopher is a lover of wisdom. As I recall my conversations with George, as I look over the wide range of subjects covered in his books, I can say, "Yes, here was a seeker of truth; here was a lover of wisdom; here was a philosopher!" Just gaze at the range of material he read, from the *Dialogues* of Plato to the mindbending stories of science fiction, from the horror of war stories to the tenderness of the poetry of love. These reading materials were often "heavy stuff," but George always understood that the voice of angels is laughter. You dare not set foot on the philosopher's path without a sense of humor. George's laughter was priceless; his mind was sharp. And he gave both as gifts to you, to me.

Over 2,000 years ago, there was a Jew who lived and worked in a Greek world. His writings occasionally reveal "Greek-like" thinking. And like George, St. Paul was a seeker . . . a searcher. He, too, delved into some pretty "heavy" subject matter. In 1 Corinthians, he blasts away at a church that is tearing itself apart because of its pride. And in one of the most beautiful pieces of literature the world has ever known, the thirteenth chapter of that letter, he writes that love is the greatest thing of all. George knew that. He lived it as well. Love radiated from him.

Also, in the same chapter, we read: "But now we see in a mirror dimly, but then face to face; now I know in part, then I shall understand fully, even as I have been fully understood." Now George is seeing face to face; he now understands fully. And what he now fully understands, what he caught a glimpse of — like seeing in a mirror dimly — is in the words of this hymn that George told me was one of his favorites . . . what he called a fight song (strangely enough, written by a neurotic German):

> *A mighty fortress is our God,*
> *A bulwark never failing;*
> *Our helper he amid the flood*
> *Of mortal ills prevailing;*
> *For still our ancient foe*
> *Doth seek to work us woe;*

His craft and power are great,
And armed with cruel hate,
On earth is not his equal.

Did we in our own strength confide,
Our striving would be losing;
Were not the right Man on our side,
The Man of God's own choosing.
Dost ask who that may be?
Christ Jesus, it is he;
Lord Sabaoth his Name,
From age to age the same,
And he must win the battle.

And though this world, with devils filled,
Should threaten to undo us;
We will not fear, for God hath willed
His truth to triumph through us;
The prince of darkness grim,
We tremble not for him;
His rage we can endure,
For lo! his doom is sure,
One little word shall fell him.

That word above all earthly powers,
No thanks to them, abideth;
The Spirit and the gifts are ours
Through him who with us sideth.
Let goods and kindred go,
This mortal life also;
The body they may kill:
God's truth abideth still,
His kingdom is forever. Amen.

Death Hurts; God Heals

Beth E. Wieseman

SETTING: *This sermon was preached at the funeral of a man, aged sixty-eight, who died suddenly of a heart attack. He was a faithful church member.*

TEXT: *Romans 8:38-39*

Death is a part of life. We say that so glibly until it hurts us. We have been separated before, but we've always come back together again. We have suffered pain before, but none so intense and deep as this. We have mourned before, but not as we do today.

We have come together to mourn, to share our grief, and look for comfort. One man among us has died unexpectedly, and we are shocked by the realization that we are not as strong and invulnerable as we like to think. This time it's happened to us, not to someone else. We feel the loss of husband, father, grandfather, friend. We are not concerned or worried about him. He is with God now, as he was all through his life. We can trust and believe that.

We gather to remember, to share our memories of who he was, and what he did. We remember how he looked, his manner of speaking, the stories he told, and the things he did that stamped him as an individual. We recall the times we spent with him, happy occasions, sad and serious ones, too. We shared many different experiences, some as fresh and new as last week, others that go back a lifetime.

All of it is part of our remembering. All those memories and images come to mind whether we want them to or not. They bring pleasure and happiness because we cared about him. He meant something to us; our memories tell us that. He left a mark on our lives where his life and ours touched at so many points. It is good and right and appropriate to remember that.

It is also very painful. We cannot add to those memories any more. They've been abruptly cut off because our relationship with him in this world is ended. His death leaves an emptiness, a great wound in our lives. No one can fill it in or cover it over.

We are left with our sorrow and grief, questions and doubts and confusion, and some anger that we are left behind. We have been hit sharply, harshly, and it hurts. It is good and right and appropriate to acknowledge these feelings also. We are glad that he does not suffer. But we are also unhappy, confused, sad, and angry that we have to go on living without him.

To say that is to be honest. We have a mixture of feelings that need to be recognized. But that is not all there is to be said. For that, we have to look beyond ourselves. We look not to a place or a thing, but to God. He created and preserves our lives. He sent his Son to us, allowed him to experience death as we do, and then raised Jesus from the dead. Because he lives, we too shall live.

If we had only memories, only ourselves to trust in, only our grief and sorrow to fill our lives, there would be no point in going on. None of that is enough to build a life on. But we are not left only to ourselves. We can turn to our God now as we have turned to him before. We know him as the Lord of life who defeated death once and for all.

We have needed the assurance of his presence before, that living presence that stays with us and cares for us no matter what happens. We need that assurance now more than ever. And we have it. St. Paul puts it this way: "For I am certain of this: neither death nor life, no angel, no prince, nothing that exists, nothing still to come, not any power, or height or depth, nor any created thing, can ever come between us and the love of God made visible in Christ Jesus our Lord." (Romans

8:38-39, The Jerusalem Bible) We can trust and depend on that love in the midst of our grief. God cared for this man. He continues to care for us now. He offers comfort in the nearness of his presence. We can call to him out of our pain, confusion, and anger. He will hear and bring healing.

Our pain will not go away today or tomorrow. God will be there; he does not go away either. He offers us light in the midst of the darkness where we live now, security when our world lies around us in pieces, and a love that is not subject to death. He is with us now, giving us strength to go on, helping us to hold on when that is all we can do, assuring us of his care and compassion. We can be sure he knows the depth of our sorrow. He knows and understands what we are feeling even when we can't put it into words.

He sends us comfort in the nearness of his loving presence, in the presence of family and friends who share our grief and care for us, and in his word. That word is "hope," hope that nothing and no one can stand between us and him. It is a promise that he will be faithful to us now as he has been before. It is Jesus Christ, our Lord, the Word in human form.

Hear and trust and believe what God has said in Jesus' life, death, and resurrection: that our lives are infinitely precious to him; that death is not the end of our relationship with God, but a new beginning of that eternal life we entered at our baptism. That life can never be taken away from us.

We will remember and discover both pain and joy in the remembering. We will weep for the man who is no longer with us, and for ourselves. But we also can and will trust in the God who will wipe away all our tears, in whom all of us, living and dead, have life now and forever. Amen.

STORIES OF

SUICIDE AND TRAGEDY

A Time To Mourn And To Celebrate

Dr. A. Roger Gobbel

SETTING: *This sermon was preached at the funeral of Stephen Broquist, a young man who was killed in the Viet Nam war. Steve had been a student at the University of Illinois in the years I was campus pastor there.*

TEXT: *Ecclesiastes 3*

A young man is dead. Loved and respected, a cherished son and friend, possessor of fine abilities and a promising future, one who loved and respected his own life — Steve is dead. That stark, dreadful, and cruel reality has brought us together, in this place, on this day.

It is for us to mourn, and rightly so. But not only that, it is for us to celeL.ate and give thanks. Think it not strange that mourning and celebrating may walk hand-in-hand. The author of the Book of Ecclesiastes was both right and wrong in something he said. You will remember he wrote:

> For everything there is a season and a time for every matter under heaven: a time to be born, and a time to die; a time to weep, and a time to laugh; a time to mourn, and a time to dance.

Things and events may well have their seasons. Yet our deepest emotions and feelings cannot be set off separately in little boxes bound by time. Our experiences, emotions, and feelings flood over each other, present all at the same time, engulfing us with both the anguish and the joy of life. We mourn and celebrate, both at the same time.

We mourn for that one who has been taken from us — knowing and feeling sorrow and sadness, bewilderment and confusion, hurt and even anger. Knowing and feeling, yet we cannot understand. Why Steve? Why a young man who could have brought so many possibilities into fruition? I don't know. In the easy answers that some might give to us — the will of God or a call to a higher purpose — there is no comfort at all. The hollow sounds of easy answers belong to those who wish not to weep and mourn. But it is right and proper for us to do so. In the presence of a cruel reality and in the anguish of our bewilderment, hurt, and even anger we mourn for one who did not have time enough to accomplish all that might have been possible.

And we weep for ourselves. Steve no longer walks among us. Throughout the length of our days, we know that our lives shall be a little less than what they might **have been. In Steve's death, we have lost something of** our own lives. It is our time of weeping and mourning.

But for the same reasons that we mourn, we can celebrate and give thanks. In ways known to each of us, Steve shared his life with us. His love, his kindness, his words, his helpfulness, his sense of joy and excitement, his Christian faith, his presence — he touched our lives with his life. Our lives have been made richer and fuller because a young man crossed our paths, desiring and daring to share his life with us. We can mourn that he will no longer cross our paths, but we can only celebrate and give thanks for life he gave to us.

Several years ago a popular folk song asked, "How many roads must a man go down before you can call him a man?" Well, I don't know the answer to that question, but I do know that Steve had walked enough to be called "a man." You see, within the last year, I was privileged to have a number of conversations with him. We talked of his hopes and plans. We talked about himself. I was always struck with the profound conviction that Steve knew who he was.

He was excited about his own life and experienced joy in his daily living. He had an abiding and active love and respect for others. He knew that meanness, pettiness, and hurt were frequent invaders of life. He was committed to the care and love of others. He knew what it meant to be a son. He reflected upon his years at home and upon all that is involved in the parent-child dynamic. He was proud to be the son of his parents. He spoke of them with profound respect, love, and thankfulness. He respected and appreciated himself as a young man. His life was rich and full. And though we may be tempted to say so, Steve would never have thought of his relatively short life in any way as a "waste." That which was exciting and enjoyable, marked by love and concern, can never be a waste.

In one of our conversations, Steve spelled out what was at the center of his life. "I know that I belong to the Lord! I know that regardless of what happens to me, I belong to the God ,nat we know in Jesus!" He was not trying to sound spiritual or pious — that was not Steve's manner. With the simplicity of directness, he has shared with us his faith and conviction. He knew who he was. "I know that I belong to the Lord!" In that knowledge and conviction, he dared to be excited about his life; he dared to enjoy his life; he dared to share his life with others. We can celebrate the life of one who knew who he was. We can rejoice and give thanks that his faith is shared with us!

It is a time for weeping and mourning, but it is also a time for celebrating and giving thanks for a young man who has crossed our paths, who graciously shared his life with us and who lived in the conviction that he belonged to the Lord. And we can leave this place in the same sure and certain knowledge that in death, as in life, Steve belongs to the Lord, and what God did to Jesus he will do to Steve also. Let us rejoice and be glad!

Hope In The Lord

Frank A. Kantz

SETTING: *This sermon was preached at the funeral of a teenager who was killed in an automobile accident. His father is a member of the Campus Ministry Directing Committee at Indiana University of Pennsylvania.*

TEXTS: Ecclesiastes 3:1-8
John 11:25

The author of the Book of Ecclesiastes has written that there is a time and a season for everything under the sun, and certainly this is a time for tears and a season for sorrow. But it is a time for worship and for proclamation as well. We have come together this morning for the funeral of a young man, Robert Zundel, whose death was sudden and tragic. His loss has left us stunned, and we find ourselves reeling under its impact, searching for some solid ground, some landmark on a sinking and drastically altered landscape. In our worship this morning there is such a landmark, such a point of reference. The cross of Jesus Christ occupies the center of our attention. This symbol of suffering and death is special because it served as the throne for the Son of God. Bob and his grief-stricken family and friends do not occupy the center stage in our drama because this is a Christian service. Its total focus is Jesus the Christ, the crucified and resurrected Son of God.

Let us make no mistake about what is happening here. We do not focus on Christ to distract ourselves from the reality of death. No. We are quite convinced that it is real; our joy has been turned into mourning. Warren and Shirley know that their son is gone. Their hopes and dreams for him have been shattered for no understandable reason . . . on an empty highway, in the middle of the night. Kevin and Susan are well aware that their brother will no longer be with them . . . sharing their problems, their fears, their thoughts, and their joys. All of the rest of us know that we have lost someone whom we loved. Each of us has tasted the bitterness of this tragic death. Therefore, we are not interested in covering it with a sugar coating of easy answers or pious platitudes.

We turn our attention to the cross of Christ because we have discovered that, through pain, we find comfort; and that through death we come to know the meaning of life. We in the church are a fellowship that has been called together by a God who lives among us, who is bone of our bone, flesh of our flesh. We are women and men who have tasted death with our Lord in the waters of baptism, who live in hope and expectation on this side of the empty tomb.

At the center of our worship and proclamation is the Lord who knows our sorrow, who has drunk deeply from the cup of our bitterness. He knows our pain and shares in our distress. We are free, then, to express our true feelings to him. At the foot of the cross we can let go, tasting the salty tang of our tears as they roll down our cheeks. In Christ we discover that we can call upon God and vent our anger, disappointment, and grief . . . without fearing that he will not understand or accept our honesty. The masks can be let down. We can weep. Our tears mingle with those from the heart of God himself. In our Christ-centered grief, we realize that the heart of God aches with the tragedy of death; and in the presence of such an outpouring of love and compassion, we are made whole again. We are able to face life without someone for whom we cared. The tears of our loving God heal the hurt within each of us.

As our tears mingle with those of God, so do they mix with those in this fellowship — the church, the body of Christ gathered to worship in his name. It is more appropriate for us to come together in this sanctuary than in some rented parlor. It was in a sanctuary like this that Bob first passed from death to life through the waters of Holy Baptism. It was in the church that Bob was nurtured by the Word of God that we proclaim today. It was here that he partook of the Body and Blood of Christ. The Body of Christ took him into itself as the church militant years ago; it accepted him into the church triumphant on Saturday morning.

It was in the church that Bob learned that God loves him. While always remaining a sinner, he, like us, has been called to sainthood in Jesus Christ. He had a constant companion in our Lord. Even in that solitary experience of his death, Bob was not alone. We will never know exactly what happened on that dark highway this past weekend, but we do know that as Christ walked with Bob throughout his life, so, too, he accompanied him on his last journey. Bob never knew any separation from the love of God. As he reached out for someone to help guide him on that new path through the portal of death, Bob felt the presence and strength of hands made rough through the hard labor of carpentry, hands pierced by the nails of Calvary. He felt the presence and comfort of another young man who also died before his time so that we might not be left alone in our own time of trial . . . so that we might be enabled to speak of the promise of life in God, even in the midst of the reality of death. Bob knew the comforting presence of Jesus Christ. The Lord who had accepted him and named him as his own years ago went with him where no one else could walk.

Just as Bob was not left alone to face death, neither are we alone as we experience grief and the bittersweetness of life. Our emphasis on the cross of Christ is only made possible by the reality that an instrument of death and torture has been made into the key that has unlocked the door of the tomb . . . forever. Death is forever destroyed. So we look forward to that moment when his kingdom will dawn in its fullness, when the grief and separation shall end, the time when God will wipe away our tears.

Until that kingdom comes, we wait with great expectation and hope . . . weeping with those who weep and mourning with those who mourn. During the interim, we play a special role in the lives of all those women and men, in Christ, who have experienced the pain of death. Right now, each of us has an important role to play in the life of the Zundel family, and it must continue throughout the long grief process. Today they need us. Tomorrow they will need us. We dare not desert them today or in the days to come. We need not ever be afraid of speaking about Bob. Indeed, we must share our sense of loss with them. They must not be left to think that they are alone in their feelings. The cross and the Word of God bring into existence a community of support and comfort for those who mourn. We are a part of that community. Our ministry to Zundels has only begun. You who are friends of Susan and Kevin: you have a task of loving and supporting them. Share their burden. Do not underestimate the power of your sincerity or sell short the value of your concern. We do not have to be afraid of those who grieve. On the contrary, we do need to reach out to them in love. We do need to walk with them — even if there is little left for us to say.

So, we have gathered together in this the season of sorrows and this time for tears. Together we have faced the reality of death at the foot of the cross of Christ. Even though we will leave sorrowful, we are filled with joy and hope for our brother Bob and his family. We are the body of Christ, the disciples of the one who put his own life on the line for us, and said, "I am the resurrection and the life; he who believes in me, though he die, yet shall he live!" (John 11:25) May that promise give you peace.

STORIES FOR

OTHER OCCASIONS

If A Man Die

Theodore C. Mayer

SETTING: *This sermon was preached on Easter, 1976, during the morning service.*

TEXT: *If a man die, shall he live again?* [Job 14:14a]

I am happy to be a minister. In fact, these past forty-five years, I would not have traded positions with a person in any other occupation. During these forty-five years of ministry, there is one thing that has changed drastically, and that is the open and interested approach that we now have toward death. It used to be the case that the minister was the only one who talked about death. Everybody else soft-pedaled "death talk." It was an uncouth subject to bring up in polite society. We shunned it. We suppressed it. We did not face up to it. So, I am pleased that in the current season, and today, we are facing death with a fresh openness that I have never experienced.

This fresh openness, and "death" as a household topic of conversation, has been made possible through the efforts of Dr. Elisabeth Kubler-Ross. It is her numerous books which have created a great interest in the subject of coping with death. Several months ago she was invited to the Kent State campus. Her original purpose for being on campus was to speak to a class of twenty students and a group of the Kent clergy. That original purpose was altered. You see, a number of other students and faculty got wind of the fact that she was to be on campus. The result: 2,000 students and faculty carpeting the Grand Ballroom to hear about death and dying. One begins to realize the appeal of the subject especially when you can get students in that number to pack auditorium and hallways. Seeing the response to Dr. Kubler-Ross, and hearing her insights, made me realize that it is high time that we in the ministry speak more with our own people about death. I do this today.

Job once asked, "If a man die, shall he live again?" It is a two-pronged question. It is a question that is found in every sob in times of bereavement. But how strange to say "if" — "if a man die!" There is no "if." All of us die sooner or later. Having just passed my 70th birthday, I am approaching that "later" category. I have to face death.

Yet a more exact interpretation of the question asked in Job would be to say, "When a man dies, will he live again?" Is life possible after death? Yes. And I was pleased to have support from the academic community. Dr. Ross stated, as a fact, that based on her scientific research of what takes place at death, there is an afterlife. I was almost at the point where I thought, "Well she is going farther than I would go on the subject!" Because, you see, I have always approached it as a matter of faith. I believe in the projection that there is a life after death in the life everlasting. And so this morning, I want to soar like a broad jumper . . . run along what I believe to be facts . . . and then take this "leap of faith" into the future.

I want to say four things about what I believe happens after this incident which we call "death" occurs.

1. I believe the transition from this life to the afterlife is immediate.

2. I believe that the afterlife is a spiritual existence; and if spirit is hard for you to digest, try personality.

3. I believe it is a time where recognition, remembrance and personal identification is possible.

4. I believe it is a place of growth.

Now let us jump into these four projections of life after death.

The first, as I indicated, is: *I believe that it is immediate.* I believe that death is the comma in the sentence of life. There is a pause. Then you go on. I think death is a stop light on the road of life. You obediently stop. But then the light changes. You go on. I believe that the afterlife comes immediately after the current life. It is like going to bed at night here and waking up the next morning there.

When Jesus was hanging on the cross, he said to the thief, "Today both of us are going to be in Paradise." Now I don't find Jesus making mistakes in any category. I do not think he was mistaken when he uttered these words. I reject that theory because, to me, that implies that God tampers with this human spirit (which is like unto his) and deep-freezes it until the final resurrection day. I do not believe he does this. I think the human spirit is so precious in God's sight that when it is not housed in this physical body, it is housed in a spiritual body –– which God provides immediately.

It is like standing on Lake Erie's shore and watching a ship crossing the lake. It becomes a speck, and your partner next to you says, "There she goes!" But where? It is only a speck in our eyes, but it is still the same ship, and on some other shore, somebody at that very moment is saying, "Here she comes!" To me that is dying.

The second thing I wish to say about dying is that *I believe it is a spiritual existence.* The Apostle Paul indicates that we put on a spiritual body — which God gives us. This may be hard for us to interpret because we are so dependent on the physical body. But remember what Jesus also said from the cross, "Father, into thy hands I commend my spirit." Jesus had a firm conviction that there was body and spirit. And I think the resurrection was a spiritual resurrection which made it possible for him to be in Emmaus, in the Upper Room, and at the Sea of Galilee.

I saw my mother at St. Luke's Hospital just before death. She was love, affection, concern, interest . . .

she was my mother. I saw her again about one half hour after death. There was only a body . . . no love, affection, concern, interest — no response. And I did not care to see that body again, because it was not my mother. And when we lowered her into the grave, my father tapped the casket and said, "Thank God we do not have to think of mother as being in there." Well, I say, Thank God. This physical body houses a spirit. But after it gives up, our spirits do not have to give up.

I believe that identification, personality, recognition, remembrance are a part of the afterlife. I just cannot accept that the spirit of man seeps into the spirit of God.

Jesus said, "In my Father's house are many mansions. I go to prepare a place for you." He says, "you." It is not a "blah." It is a "you" personality. It is a remembrance, a recognition of "you." Remember Jesus in the garden was not immediately recognized by Mary. But then, when he spoke her name, she knew he was Jesus. The two men on the road were not aware that Jesus was with them until he broke bread. Their eyes were opened. Recognition.

Yes, I think there is recognition and remembrance. I do not place much of an emphasis on dreams. But I had a dream that, at least for me, interpreted what I am trying to say. I died and, egotistical as I am, I landed up in heaven. Some might question the dream right from the start. But there I was. It was a lovely place . . . like the *"Sound of Music"* in the Austrian Alps. And I was walking along when I saw a solitary figure, at quite a distance, running toward me. I was sure it was somebody to welcome me. As the figure came closer, I saw it was a young man, perhaps in his early thirties. I suddenly recognized this young man as my father. Now my father was going on forty when I was born; I only remember him as a man from fifty to eighty. But here was my father at thirty. He was greeting me. At least to me, this is a glimpse into eternity . . . because I believe that there is remembrance, recognition, and individuality!

And finally, *I believe it is a place of growth!* I suppose we ministers are guilty of creating a clergyman's heaven — streets of gold, pearly gates, and people playing harps ... sort of a combination between a rest home and a conservatory of music (where harp is the only instrument that is played). Again, you know, my reaction as a boy was "horrors!" This is a confession. I did not worry about getting into heaven. I worried about what I would do in heaven. I was not interested in sitting around in a rocking chair, like the green benches in St. Petersburg, for eternity. I was not interested in playing a harp. But that is a farce. That's hell! Heaven is a place of growth.

Where are you the happiest? You are the happiest when you are creating, and learning, and growing, and living — not when you are on an eternal vacation, resting. Would God make heaven worse than this earth? No! Death is not going to make us much wiser than we are at the moment; and most of us will wake up in heaven "just as dumb" as we are at the moment. But think of the possibilities in an environment where we are able to lear , to live, to grow, and to love. That for me is heaven. And that is the type of projection that I see as I look into the future.

A minister was calling on a friend in the hospital. The friend was dying. He wanted to have some indication about the afterlife. He said to the minister, "Tell me what heaven is like." That is an awfully hard question to answer in a few moments. While he was thinking, the minister heard a scratching on the hospital room door. He recognized the barks of his little dog. He had left the dog out in his parked car. But the dog had chased him into the hospital, down the hallway, and to this room. So the minister said, "Do you hear that bark and the scratching on the door?" "Yes." "That is my little dog. He has never been in this hospital. He doesn't know what is on this side of that door. He knows only one thing: I am here. And when I open the door, you will see how happy he is. What a welcome he will give me when he bounds through the door."

So, I have shared my humble thoughts with you. And I have had to be honest about my ignorance . . . but I think heaven is a place where Jesus is content to be. That is about all I need to know. I think it will be a joyous experience meeting him! Amen.

Death: A New Responsibility

Allen Myrick

SETTING: *The sermon was preached to a local congregation on the first Sunday after Easter.*

TEXTS: *1 Kings 17:10-23*
2 Corinthians 5:1-10

Death is much in fashion in some circles today: many people take great interest in it. Books are being written about death, and they sell widely. Movies which make Death the main character have done very well, movies like *Earthquake* and *Towering Inferno* and *Jaws.* The tourist trade in Rumania should flourish this summer, when many will visit the home of Count Dracula. Colleges teach courses in death, and special lectures and seminars are well attended. We take great interest in death these days. Perhaps one reason for this is that death has become a new responsibility in our time.

Now we are not accustomed to death being a responsibility. *Life* is our responsibility — we're quite busy enough with that, thank you. And over the centuries we have found ways to get someone else to take responsibility for death. That is what we hire soldiers for: they deal out death, when we think it is necessary. That is what undertakers are for: they will look after death so that we do not have to think about it. That is the job of the doctor: to step in when death threatens, and take care of things for us. That is the role of the church: to say the right words in the presence of death, to set the right mood, lifting that responsibility from us.

The woman is our Old Testament reading (1 Kings 17:10-23) seemed to feel this way. She and her son had struggled through a long and terrible drought, saving every morsel, rationing every drop of water, clinging stubbornly to life. And when the boy became critically ill, the mother did not want to take responsibility for this. She had worked so hard to cope with life that she did not want to cope with death, too! So she turned to the prophet, the "professional." "You take over," she says to him, "you deal with this dying boy. He is your problem now!"

We do not want the responsibility for life. Isn't it enough that we have to die ourselves, some day? And we are comforted, perhaps, by the reminder of George Buttrick: ". . . each of us must die each for himself, and none of us is asked to die more than once. All who have lived before us seem to have managed the business of dying with at least this measure of success: they are dead." But in our time there has been a change, hasn't there? We have to make decisions about death, as well as life.

Medical technology has helped to create this new responsibility. The combination of testing and surgery and drugs and complex machines and superb training means that some people can be kept alive almost indefinitely now. And the question arises, "Should they be kept alive?" That question thrusts new responsibility upon us.

Part of that responsibility lies in the question, "Who shall decide?" When treatment must be prescribed for you, or for me, or for someone we love — and when one kind of treatment can prolong life and another kind shorten or end it — who makes that decision? This question was raised quite clearly in a case I knew of not long ago. A man was very old, going blind, with no desire to live anymore. He had a heart attack, and was rushed to the Emergency Room. From then on, he had nothing to say about what happened, for he was unconscious. His family was not really consulted about treatment, for in the rush of the hospital, doctors told the family, "He has got to go to Intensive Care." The family was not asked, but told, and what could they say? Once there, machines were attached, monitors were set up, a staff took over which is trained to do anything possible to keep the patient alive. The doctors and medical technology decided.

But should the decision be made this way? I have great respect for the medical profession, and for nearly all the doctors I have dealt with over the years. But I do not believe that they alone should decide what kind of treatment should be given. These are decisions which should be shared with the family and the patient.

One of the basic principles of medical care is "informed consent." This means that at each step in the diagnosis and the treatment, the patient or the family is consulted. They are told the known facts and the possible next steps, and family and patient help make the decisions. If we really value human life and respect the freedom and dignity of other people, this kind of sharing should happen, especially when matters of life and death are involved.

And if, as sometimes happens, the patient is too sick to be consulted, or is not even conscious, this simply underscores our need to think through beforehand how we feel. We here today, whether we are young or old, healthy or sick, need to decide how we wish to be treated, if there is no reasonable expectation of our recovery from disability. And we need to tell those close to us of our decision. For we share responsibility for our own death, as we do for our life. Dying is a part of living. What happens to me when I am near death is *my business*. Since I have responsibility for my *life*, under God, that responsibility covers my *death* as well.

How shall we decide, if it comes to a question of living or dying? What are the principles which should guide us? There are several, but let me mention only two, which occupy a central place in the Christian tradition.

One is the importance of the *way* we die. I sometimes think that we have so isolated death from the rest of life, we have put the process of dying so much out of our sight, so much out of our homes, so much out of our experience, that we may be overlooking how the very process of dying can be significant for others. It can be a kind of witness for others. For perhaps the most important thing about our lives is not what *happens* to us, but how we *deal* with what happens to us. The way people deal with death can have peculiar power for other people.

We know this is true of the great heroes and heroines. Fiction is full of noble deaths which inspire others: "It is a far, far better thing that I do than I have ever done," says Sydney Carton at his death. Real life has produced many persons who have changed the course of history through the way they died: Christians need not be reminded of this, just nine days after Good Friday. But have you thought how *your* death — the way you deal with your death — can give meaning and hope to others? There is no guarantee that it will, for none of us can control how death will come; but the possibility exists.

I remember a woman who died about five years ago. There was nothing dramatic about her death. There was no great crisis, as there is with some kinds of illness. She was in her eighties, and death came slowly, through a long decline. Her energy began to diminish. She could not go out of the house anymore. She had a number of falls which made her weaker. The aches and pains of old age increased, and she was confined to one or two rooms. She was in the hospital several times, but that did not really solve anything.

She was really dying over a period of a year or two. But there was always a grace about her. She kept a kind of inner dignity. She had a sense of humor about herself and her pain. I always felt better when I had been to see her.

She died one summer, a few weeks before her older son was to go on an extended trip abroad. She did not die of anything in particular; she just sort of wore out. Her son was convinced that she had made up her mind to die then, and not any later, for later he would be gone, and would have to rush back for her funeral. She did not want to be a nuisance, he said, so she died when she did. Perhaps he was right, who knows? It was the kind of person she was. The way she died enriched those around her, just as her life had.

This is not always possible, for death comes in many ways, and none of us can control how it comes. But we can hope that the way we die may be consistent with the best of what we believe in. We can make clear to others our wish that when death is near, nothing should be done to prevent us from dying with grace and love.

We can also live each day in ways which give God glory, and which open ourselves to God's grace. For if we live by God's grace, perhaps we can also die in God's grace, and even reveal his grace to others as we die. Alan Paton put it very well, in his beautiful book, *For You Departed.** It is a book about his wife's death of cancer, and his re ponse to her dying. He writes:

> Lord, give me grace to die in Thy will.
> Prepare me for whatever place or condition awaits
>   me.
> Let me die true to those things I believe to be true.
> And suffer me not through any fear of death to fall
>   from Thee.
>
> Lord, give me grace to live in Thy will also.
> Help me to master any fear, any desire, that
>   prevents
> me from living in Thy will. Make me, O Lord, the
>   instrument

of Thy peace, that I may know eternal life.

Into Thy hands I commend my spirit.

The other thing I ask you to remember, as you consider the responsibility of death, is that *death is not the end.* Christ lives! He is risen from the dead. So we shall live. When death comes to us we shall be raised from death with him. In our reading from 2 Corinthians, Paul puts it even more strongly: he says that life after we die is to be preferred this life. He says that when he is anxious, it is a result of his being eager to join Christ in eternity. This does not mean that Paul hated life or wanted to escape its responsibilities. On the contrary, he loved life, he lived it with enthusiasm, he taught that each day is given us that we may please God. But Paul knew that because Christ was raised from death, we too shall be raised. Our goal in life is not to survive, not to be healthy, not to live a long life; our goal is to please God as long as we live, in the faith that we shall live with him forever.

So, however we deal with death, whatever mistakes we may make when others are dying, however badly we may behave when our own death comes, death does not separate us from God. We may fear death, for it is unknown, and it ends much that we love. But it need not be a cold and ugly fear. It need not be an ultimate fear. The resurrection of Christ makes clear that death is under God's rule. Death is one of the many paths which lead to God.

I know of no one who has made this clearer than James Weldon Johnson, in his poem, *Go Down Death.*** The poem speaks of "Sister Caroline" on her death-bed, and of God's summoning his servant Death to go and fetch her for him:

And God said: Go down, Death, go down,
Go down to Savannah, Georgia . . .

And find Sister Caroline.
She's borne the burden and heat of the day,
She's labored long in my vineyard,
And she's tired ⎯
She's weary ⎯
Go down, Death, and bring her to me.

While we were watching round her bed,
She turned her eyes and looked away,
She saw what we couldn't see;
She saw Old Death. She saw Old Death
Coming like a falling star.
But Death didn't frighten Sister Caroline;
He looked to her like a welcome friend.
And she whispered to us: I'm going home,
And she smiled and closed her eyes.

And Death took her up like a baby,
And she lay in his icy arms,
But she didn't feel no chill.
And Death began to ride again ⎯
Up beyond the evening star,
Out beyond the morning star,
Into the glittering light of glory,
On to the Great White Throne.
And there he laid Sister Caroline
On the loving breast of Jesus.

*Alan Paton, For You Departed, © Charles Scribner's Sons. Used with permission.

**"Go Down Death" From God's Trombones by James Weldon Johnson. Copyright 1927 by the Viking Press, Inc., © renewed 1955 by Grace Nail Johnson. Reprinted by permission of The Viking press.

ARTICLES FOR

REFLECTION

From Denial To Affirmation

George W. Gaiser

In four years of teaching classes on death at a university noted in our time for death, Kent State, I have become convinced of one thing: denial of death is at least as strong as those all writing about death indicate it to be!

One can point in my community to the aftermath of the May 4, 1970, tragedy. The one thing on which more people from diverse segments of the school and community agree than any other is "that we might forget that day!" Part of that sentiment is an overt denial that four real live people became four real dead people on that tumultuous occasion. That kind of basic denial is bad enough simply because it is so unrealistic. The tragedy is compounded in that such a community is doomed to a constant "instant replay" of that one lovely, yet oh-so-ugly spring afternoon!

Individually, I find students and their teachers no better off. On one memorable occasion I argued until I was exhausted (and that's a long time!) with a health center doctor the advisability of telling a graduating senior that he was dying of Leukemia. In utter frustration she finally blurted out, "Maybe you can handle the idea of your death, but I can't!" Whether she was right about me is of little consequence. Of great consequence was the artificial atmosphere which her denial created at that one moment in a person's life when, more than at any other, the situation called for the openness to be really close.

Probably at no point is this denial I am talking about better illustrated than in the case of a young lady of about twenty. In nearly every new class there is one student who will state in the face of incredible statistical evidence to the contrary, "I'm going to beat the odds. I will not die." In the case in question, that denial was so strong that the woman exclaimed, "I'm never going to get any older than I am now!"

General examples from scenes observed in random glances at society abound. How old is the average age of a TV commercial actor or actress? Even if over fifty, the object inevitably is that by taking "Toiler's Tonic" one will be assured of feeling and acting twenty. Why is Florida the geriatric clinic it is? Is it simply because the climate is warm, or is there a convenience about it which enables us to get those old folks out of sight so that they do not remind us that we are mortal, will grow old, and even die? What about our strict avoidance of pain by any means licit or illicit? Can we not accept that there is a dark side of life which must be faced if we are to have anything like a whole understanding of human existence?

Move to a funeral establishment, any funeral establishment. What words do we inevitably hear at the side of the coffin, even in the face of the stark reality of a person through whose arteries the blood no longer pulses? The ubiquitous, "Doesn't he look natural?" If you substitute "good" or "life-like," for "natural," I can't remember a funeral I've attended or conducted where, at one point, that phrase will not have been heard. In addition, the concealing we do with cosmetics in life spills over into death. The result is an abysmally crude attempt at denial even when face-to-face with the dead person. It is as if, like Moses on Sinai, some of the aura will rub off on us. Except that it is not light, it is darkness from which we would hide behind the cosmetic veil.

The reason all of these examples strike home is that they are overt manifestations of that deep-seated, motivational denial so basic to late 20th century America. Many of its symptoms are not so obvious; they lie under the surface. The purpose of this article is not to bring up all of those, but to ask what we, as the

Christian Church, can do about it? How can we reverse the trend? What is a positive way for revolution in the best sense, turning the situation upside down?

Unfortunately, we must, as a church, begin where we are. In an article in *Catholic Exponent* (February 7, 1975), Elisabeth Kubler-Ross (the "death-and-dying" lady) suggests that people "who sound religious are not the truly religious ones. The people who talk about the afterlife are denying death. They never face the reality that you have to die before the Resurrection." I understand and am sympathetic with what she is talking about. For a long time, Christianity has been abetting the denial syndrome through a cheap understanding of Resurrection which is nothing more than a shallow reading of Greek immortality dressed up for followers of the Jew from Nazareth. It is as firm a denial of death as we find on TV or in the funeral parlor. We shall not all die, we shall all "pass on," go home, etcetera, ad nauseam! I attended a funeral purported to be Christian in which the word "death" would not have been mentioned at all were it not for the necessity of reading from Scripture!

Do we believe in the "immortality of the soul," or do we, as the Creed suggests (probably over against the very tendency in its time which we note in ours), believe in the "resurrection of the body?" Perhaps more importantly, how can we make resurrection once more meaningful for people influenced not only by a secular world dedicated to denial, but a church hung up in watered-down Greek philosophical thought? Is there a way which is not so radical that it destroys more than it creates?

Let me suggest that there is at least a basic contradiction with which we can begin. While we talk volumes about immortality, we still do confess that position of the Creed to which I alluded earlier. Sooner or later the most undisturbed "soul" (see "psyche") must ask itself what that Third Article phrase means, else death's reign is absolute. Sooner or later the most "status quo" Christian in the most dogmatic of denominations, repeating the Second Article, has to think about the words "suffered, crucified, dead, buried, descended into hell." Jesus really did die! That is not a sham. I have not been confessing all these years that the Lord "passed away" or "easily went through the gauzy curtain into eternal life." He died!

Ruminating on that contradiction, one can perhaps get in touch with his own deep-gut conviction, even if in fear, that in spite of all the denial-mechanisms brought into play (some of which may even be a temporary necessity psychologically), despite all notions of immortality to the contrary, "I know that I shall die. It was no sham for Jesus and it is no sham for me. The spectre is there, waiting at the end of my life, and the scythe is sharp!"

It is a very frightening spectre. No amount of belief adequately stills that fear. But bravery is not the absence of fear, bravery is action in the face of fear. Where shall we get strength for that bravery? That is the proper question for us, even as it was for Jesus.

It is at this point that an analogy is helpful, at least for me. Is it coincidental that two phrases occur back-to-back in the Creed? Before we say, "resurrection of the body," we say, "forgiveness of sins." What is the connection and how is it significant here in terms of denial and death?

Think with me for a moment about the dynamics of forgiveness. How do we stand before God? Is it still, as it was for the Psalmist, "If thou Lord shouldst mark iniquities, O Lord, who shall stand?" If it is, then it is not that in forgiveness God "picks up the pieces." It is that he re-creates. That gives meaning to our notion of Baptism which suggests that the Old Adam is drowned, dead, and that the new man springs forth. In renewing those vows repentantly day by day, we make no apology for the Old Adam's re-emergence from the baptismal waters, gasping for breath in our life. We claim, rather, the constantly refreshing and renewing power of God to create afresh that new man once again. Luther says it well when he suggests that until we are nothing, God can do nothing with us. Repentance, as a claim on God, is no claim at all. It is an admission that we are as dead men, that life is not in us, but in him.

See how nicely that fits in with, "resurrection of the body?" If we really believe in that kind of God, then Christianity's claim all along is that continuity for creation, for the race, and for each of us as individuals is not innate in it or in us, continuity resides in him. As it is true for us in forgiveness day by day, so is it also true for us at our death. We die. God lives! We can quit the denial business, at least as a way of life we can. We know that God is a God of life. Death is an enemy, ours and his. God is victorious over death; its power has been destroyed in the very act of death, real death, on a cross. Death is beaten at its own game. Death is real, but God has the last word, as the first word. And the last word is resurrection: new life! He who creates *ex nihilo*, out of nothing, at the beginning, re-creates my life *ex nihilo* in this moment, through forgiveness, and will re-create, resurrect, if you will, new life, *ex nihilo*, out of my very real death — and yours — at life's end!

Shall we then affirm both death and resurrection? Or shall we settle for a denial which obscures death and an immortality which denies resurrection? The inexorable grace of God suggests a way for the former. And his grace is sufficient!

The Church's Role In Death Education

Donald W. Shilling

This article will test two well-attested findings, or at least reflect upon them in terms of the author's experience and several modern responses to the interests of people in the subject of death and dying. It is my hope that the current interest in death will be transformed from faddishness to the central proclamation of the Good News that is fitting to the church's role in death education.

OTHERWORLDLINESS

Forty-five years have passed since John Baillie wrote *And the Life Everlasting*. At the time of his writing he spoke of the revolt of moderns against "otherworldliness." He claimed that "the belief in an eternal world has failed and that the need for such belief has also failed."[1] Forty years later Krister Stendahl said that modern persons are not concerned with their souls, in fact they may need to be persuaded that they have one before the destiny of it may even be addressed. What moderns are "concerned about is not so much what is going to happen to (them) but what is going to happen to this poor world."[2]

One question that I have addressed to every class I have taught in the past four years, and to many church and community groups, is phrased something like this: "If you were given a choice between dying quickly (e.g., in an accident or in your sleep), or in dying a lingering death over a period of time, which would you choose?" The overwhelming answer of people of all ages and walks of life to this kind of choice is the sudden death. Some may not relish the thought of an accident, but if pressed to a decision they opt for that choice rather than dying over a period of time.

The reasons for that choice of a quick death are many, but often the aspect of a pain-free, worry-free kind of death looms large. "I don't want to suffer . . . I don't want to be a burden on my family . . . I don't want a lot of money spent on useless care, etc." are variations on this theme. In contrast to the Middle Ages when a lingering death was desired for the time it gave a person to "get right with God" there seems to be little or no anxiety concerning this aspect of dying. Respondents to my question have shown concern over the process of dying, but not over the ultimate destiny of their souls.

To this extent, at least, Baillie's observation made during the Depression — pre-World War II, the Bomb, Korean "police action," Vietnam War, and Kent State — seems supported. The world has changed, but the feeling against "otherworldliness" seems still to be with us. Perhaps one reason for this is a widespread disbelief in hell. People will talk about reincarnation, or heaven, or non-being, but most persons whom I have polled in the recent past have no belief in hell. Because it does not exist "over there," life here on earth is relieved of any anxiety about it, and can be lived for its own sake.

The change in the world over the past four decades has been considerable, but probably no less so that one fundamental change discussed by both Brunner and Baillie. Brunner, for instance, notes that belief in progress is a presupposition of all human action, in that we act in order to bring about change. Yet, he also notes how for ages human existence was governed by nature. The rhythmic cycle of the seasons, the phases of the moon, and the ever-recurring patterns of living tied to those cycles were assumed to be eternal. The power to break the dependence on this conception of time and the world "was found in the revelational faith of the Israelite-Christian tradition."[3]

Believing that the world was created by God, that it has a beginning, and that it is moving toward a cosmic goal, means that world history is conceived linearly rather than cyclically. The implications of this belief are to be seen in the concept of progress which came to the fore in the 18th and 19th centuries. If all is conceived as circular, there can be no progress, because all is ever-returning. If, however, one is sustained by faith in the "transcendent freedom of the God of revelation" who creates and redeems, then the possibilities for freedom to progress are practically unlimited.[4]

Certain qualifications of the faith in progress have occured in this century. In theological thought the idea of the Kingdom of God as a "growing, developing" thing has largely been discarded. The Kingdom is viewed as God's kingly rule, his intervention and activity punctuating time, rather than the end product of a progressive development by humans. The horrendous events of this century have shattered the self-confidence of moderns in their abilities to sustain progress in more modest areas of their lives as well.

In economics the Great Depression, recessions, inflation, unemployment, and currency devaluations are among the causes of a dwindling lack of confidence that this area of life can be controlled. The belief in the goodness of humans, or at least in the progressive growth of human goodness, was shattered by totalitarian dictatorships, Auschwitz, Chilean torture of prisoners, and the numerous human rights violations that are constantly broadcast to the world. The confidence that humans can conquer the universe is challenged daily by the persistence of welfare rolls, hunger, and disease.

Freedom from dependence on the cycles of nature has been realized in the Judaeo-Christian concept of linear time, and of a Creator God who Redeems in history and in the *eschaton*. Freedom from these cycles has come in more mundane ways through heating and cooling systems, irrigation, greenhouses, and countless other technical advances. Freedom from a cyclical view means belief in progress for a time, but that belief has lately been shattered or called into question in many areas of modern life.

Bondage to an unredeemed human nature, however, has led to disillusionment, apathy, and a frantic search for "solutions" that will restore confidence. This has meant, on the other side of the discussion of Baillie's point, a great interest in the occult, astrology, Eastern religions, and the more authoritarian forms of Christian faith. What each of these has in common is a claim to provide secure answers to the disillusioned modern who has lost faith in the religion of progress. Turning to ancient witchcraft or superstitious belief such as astrology are acts of desperation on the part of moderns. Simplistic solutions, such as reliance on neo-Gnostic fundamentalism to provide saving knowledge, are sought by many moderns. Others have turned to beliefs in ever-recurring chances to "progress" through reincarnations as a source of hope. Some have simply given up and opted out via drugs, TV addiction, or other "cop-out" routes.

Each of these "other-worldly" solutions is different from the old "other-worldliness" mentioned by Baillie, with the possible exception of fundamentalism. They differ in that life in this world is not seen as determinative of the quality of life to be lived in the "other" world. To that extent they do not support Baillie's observation. They are supportive of his observation, however, in that they generally do not take this world seriously, and seek to find "answers" to the modern malaise in other-worldly authorities. The evidence which supports, and that which differs from Baillie's observation, are both pronounced. Neither position on it can be sustained without question.

SOULS OR WORLD

Not unrelated to the first observation made by Baillie is the second one as phrased by Stendahl: moderns are concerned about "not so much what is going to happen to (them) but what is going to happen to this poor world." Is it true that moderns have turned away from the Platonic soul-body dualism and the worldview it was based upon? Is it further true that moderns are more concerned with this world's future than the destiny of their individual souls? Again, I would answer both "yes" and "no" to each of these questions.

The widespread disdain for the belief in hell would say that the concern over the destiny of the soul is certainly not the same as it was. The popularity of a belief in reincarnation has all the earmarks of substituting a different "hell" for the fiery abyss. Baillie tells us that there was no reincarnation belief in India until the 6th century B.C., when the Upanishads established it as successive reincarnation "determined absolutely by the nature of (one's) deeds in (one's) previous lives."[5] The law of Karma (which is Sanskrit for deed) was Plato's law of the Deed, tied also to the transmigration of souls on the Wheel of Birth.

Although reincarnation has been basic to Buddhism, Jainism, Sikhism, and Hinduism, it has not enjoyed a wide acceptance in the West. The Orphic Wheel of Birth was seen as "oppressive consciousness that there is no end."[6] Thus, the claim that it is a substitute doom for belief in hell. Those who promote this belief today, however, see a much more hopeful quality in it.

Leslie D. Weatherhead has argued that reincarnation is nowhere denied in the Bible, and he finds hints in Scripture that it may have been accepted. He notes that it is not taught in the Bible, but that: "The early Church accepted it until the Council of Constantinople, A.D. 553, and then only discarded it by a vote in the proportion of 3 to 2."[7] He further argues that reincarnation is in harmony with Christian teachings of justice, that it makes sense, and that it supports the workings of God's will in each life "on earth as it is in heaven." Weatherhead also argues that it answers questions about genius, *deja vu*, and other unexplained phenomena.

Most belief today in reincarnation does not come from the logical reasoning of a Christian minister like Weatherhead. It is based in the *Tibetan Book of the Dead*[8] or a fascination with Eastern religions. And, if followed through in its teaching of Karma, extinction of desire, and union with the divine in *nirvana*, it fails to meet the Christian goal of communion with God. Communion, not union, is the goal of Christian teaching of repentance, grace, judgment and resurrection. Christian teaching of the redemption of the person, calls into question much of reincarnation teaching. This point needs to be made by the Church, but little is being taught in Christian churches relative to any aspect of an afterlife, much less reincarnation.

One very effective teaching on afterlife is presently coming out of the medical community, or to be more specific, out of two physicians: Raymond A. Moody, Jr., and Elisabeth Kubler-Ross. Moody's book, *Life After Life*, has caught the imagination of the American public. It is based on detailed interviews with fifty persons out of 150 that he was aware of when he wrote. He classifies the total into three distinct categories of "near death" experiences:

1. The experiences of persons who were resuscitated after having been thought, adjudged, or pronounced clinically dead by their doctors.

2. The experiences of persons who, in the course of accidents or severe injury or illness, came very close to physical death.

3. The experiences of persons who, as they died, told them to other people who were present. Later,

these other people reported the content of the death experience to me.[9]

What Dr. Moody's interviews have turned up are fifteen rather common elements of these "near death" experiences. No two persons have had identical experiences, and there is no element common to everyone, but he is able to piece together a composite picture of the experience. In a very general way it can be said that persons who have "died" have left their bodies to become spectators of the "death," and were in a state of peace and wholeness after the initial moments of uncertainty. They have met religious or family figures who helped them in the transition, and have had a life review and a meeting with a being of light that constituted a kind of judgment on their lives. This experience has removed the fear of death from them and motivated them to make positive changes in living patterns subsequent to their recovery.[10]

Dr. Ross spent a whole day, during a five-day workshop I attended in 1975, telling of similar reports from her own patients, and from privately-polled patients of other physicians in the United States and around the world. She claimed that the sum of the testimony, which is identical to the description by Moody, plus other psychic experiences she has had "prove" to her that there is life after death. (Moody does not make this claim, nor does he think it possible at this time.) She described a variety of experiences in collaboration with Robert A. Monroe.[11] Monroe's experiments with astral projection, which he labels simply as out of body experiences, caught Dr. Ross's attention at about the same time that a clinically dead patient revived and told her of an experience like that which Moody independently reported sometime later.

Moody and Kubler-Ross may not agree on what all this proves, but each has told of experiences which seem to attest to the survival of the soul after death of the body. Monroe's book supports this conclusion as well, as do certain parts of John Lilly's experiences as a "mind-explorer." [12] H. A. Williams comments on the fact that death (not Moody's "near death") by its nature gives no evidence on the question of life after because no one has returned. But, he goes on to add:

> It is true that physical research supplies evidence to a certain degree, but it is of extremely limited significance. All that can reasonably be inferred from the evidence so far available is that certain people survive death for a certain period of time. And this is not evidence for immortality, let alone immortality on a general scale. [13]

The list of books and teachings is long and impressive, ranging from well-known scientist like Lilly to the *Tibetan Book of the Dead*. Without hazarding a judgment of each or all of them in terms of their accuracy and reliability, I believe their very existence and popularity deny Stendahl's observation. People are interested and concerned with the destiny of their souls. Some believe that the evidence proves immortality of the soul, though I would agree with Williams that it does not — and I would point out that most phenomena can be explained or called into question by a somewhat different interpretation of the very science which produced the "proof."

IN CLOSING

The point of this article is not to prove or disprove the observations of Baillie and Stendahl, though I have argued that there is pretty sound evidence on both sides. Moderns have rejected the "other-worldliness" of hell, but have embraced other "other-worldly" solutions. Moderns have attested to a great interest in making life in this world more human and whole, yet have a fascination with reincarnation, physchical phenomena, and life after life. The evidence is mixed.

In many ways the situation today is as confused for the church as it was for Jesus in the time of his ministry. Perhaps we should follow his example and do little speculation about death and the afterlife, saving our energies and interst for making the present life "abundant." But the eschatological tension in Jesus' teaching shown so strongly in recent studies of the Kingdom of God, calls us to put our faith in the God of promise. We should follow the example of Paul and place death and resurrection at the center of our teaching.

Thus, I call for the church to make known its teaching on death, the resurrection, life, judgment, and the Kingdom of God. This teaching must be done with confidence and competence as a reflection of our long history of biblical and theological reflection. But it shall also be most effective when it is least dogmatic, and most open to the experiences and musings of the people being taught.

I do not believe there are any experts on death and the afterlife. Some of us have studied it in more disciplined ways than others. Some of us have thought on it longer and harder than others. Some of us may be dying, or may have had a "near death" experience, but none of us has been truly qualified by such experience to be an expert.

The subject may only be addressed in humility and thanksgiving. The most suspect "authority" on death is the one who is proud of his/her knowledge — the self-proclaimed gurus of East and West. The subject must be addressed in awe and wonder, but also in thankful celebration that death's power has been broken by the action of God in Christ. In this certainty of faith we find the church's role in death education.

Footnotes

1. (New York: Charles Scribner's Sons, 1933), page 6.

2. "Immortality Is Too Much and Too Little," in *The End Of Life*, ed. John D. Roslansky (Amsterdam/London: North Holland Publishing Company, 1973), p. 79.

3. Emil Brunner, *Eternal Hope*, trans. Harold Knight (Philadelphia: Westminster Press, 1954), pages 16 - 17.

4. Ibid.

5. Baillie, page 114.

6. Ibid., page 116.

7. Leslie D. Weatherhead, *The Case For Reincarnation* (Surry, England: M. C. Peto, 1957), page 4. Under the title "Reincarnation and Renewed Chances" the expanded substance of this lecture now forms chapter XIV of *The Christian Agnostic* (Hodder & Stoughton, 1965).

8. *The Tibetan Book Of The Dead*, trans. with commentary by Francesca Fremantle and Chogyam Trungpa, The Clear Light Series (Berkeley and London: The Shambhala Publications, 1975).

9. Raymond A. Moody, Jr., with a foreword by Elisabeth Kubler-Ross (Atlanta: Mockingbird Books, 1975), page 19. Used with permission.

10. Ibid., page 10.

11. Robert A. Monroe, *Journeys Out Of The Body* (Garden City, New York: Doubleday & Company, Anchor Press Edition, 1973).

12. John C. Lilly, *The Center of the Cyclone* (New York: Julian Press, Bantam Books Edition, 1973).

13. From *True Resurrection*, by H.A. Williams. Copyright © 1972 by H.A. Williams. Reprinted by permission of Holt, Rinehart and Winston, Publishers.

Death And Dying Profile

Victor A. Myers

A pastor and/or a congregation can provide an important ministry by establishing, for members a *Death and Dying Profile*. Such a profile seeks to accomplish two things:

1) It provides a checklist of details which can prove helpful at the time of death; and

2) It provides a "guiding statement" which reveals for pastor and family the wishes of the deceased.

The profile can be distributed during a " death and dying" seminar, at the request of members, when pastor or lay leaders visit with shut-ins, or during a counseling session. However they are distributed, I suggest that families retain one copy and the church office another copy.

Why such a profile? Because it serves two practical functions:

1) It is a tool which enables families and/or individuals to face up to the reality of death. Furthermore, it allows a person to indicate preferences, thus permitting other family members to be free from the burden of "having to guess" what the desires of the deceased were.

2) It serves as a "reminder" at a time when it is so easy to forget or become confused.

What follows is a sample of forms which can be included in the profile. It should be noted that on Form #2 (Benefits) and Form #4 (Burial Cost), no dollar amounts have been inserted; these amounts can be inserted according to your local situation. It is imperative that a congregation plan to periodically update these forms.

FORM #1
WHAT TO DO WHEN DEATH OCCURS

1. Call your pastor immediately.

2. Call a physician. His signature on the death certificate is necessary before the funeral director may move the body.

3. Call your funeral director if one has previously been selected.

4. Check all life and casualty insurance benefits, including social security, credit unions, trade unions, fraternal, military.

5. Notify all insurance companies.

6. Notify the attorney holding the will and the Executor-Executrix.

7. Check all debts and installment payments. Some may carry insurance clauses which will cancel debts. If there will be a delay in meeting payments, consult with creditors and seek an extension.

8. Notify relatives and friends.

FORM #2
BENEFITS

SOCIAL SECURITY LUMP-SUM PAYMENTS:
This payment must be formally applied for through the local Social Security Office.

The spouse is entitled to the entire lump sum benefits regardless of the cost of the funeral. This payment is also available to whomever paid the funeral expenses in the event of no surviving spouse.

FEDERAL DEATH BENEFITS FOR VETERANS AND THEIR DEPENDENTS
1. A payment ($.....) will be paid toward the burial or cremation of a veteran.

2. A grave marker is provided free through the VA for the graves of certain veterans who are buried in private cemetaries.

3. Death pensions may be available to certain widows and children of veterans (who have died of non-service connnected causes).

4. To make it easier to collect these benefits, survivors should have a record of the veteran's serial number and/or have available his discharge papers.

OTHER BENEFITS
Other forms of insurance may be available. For instance, if occupational factors were involved in the death, Workmen's Compensation may be in effect. An automobile club insurance may also be in effect.

Explore all possibilities.

FORM #3
LOCATION OF IMPORTANT PAPERS

1. Birth Certificate:
   Mr. _____

   Mrs. _____

2. Social Security Number:
   Mr. _____

   Mrs. _____

3. Marriage License _____

4. Veteran Discharge Papers _____

5. Insurance Policies _____

6. Title to Car _____

7. Deed to Property _____

8. Bank Accounts:
   Checking _____

   Savings _____

9. Stocks/Bonds _____

10. Cemetery Deed _____

11. Will _____

12. Statement of Guidance in the Event of Death _____

_____

_____

_____

FORM #4
BURIAL COST GUIDE

[*Give date and location of cost estimates.*]

1. Cremation Costs: _____

2. Casket Costs:
   Wooden Caskets _____

   Metal Caskets _____

   [*Does the price include services, use of home, use of cars, etc.?*]

3. Viewing or Visiting Hours: _____

   [*Some homes may charge a fee for the use of a room for visiting hours.*]

4. Embalming: _____

5. Make-Up, Hair-Styling, Etc.: _____

6. Transportation Fees: _____

7. Grave Opening: _____

8. Death Certificates: $2 for each one that is needed. The number needed depends on the number of

insurance companies and other agencies/offices which require them.

9. Flowers: Price range varies. Casket spray begins at $50 and goes up from that figure.

10. Burial Lots: Vary, depending on cemetery and date of purchase; sometimes location within the cemetery may make a difference.

11. Vault: May or may not be required by the cemetery. Be certain to determine if it is a metal or cement vault that is required.
Metal _____

Cement _____

FORM #5
GUIDING STATEMENT

1. Name: _____
           (last)   (first)   (middle)

   Address: _____

   Telephone: _____

2. I would like the following person(s) to have charge of the arrangements:
   1st Choice: _____ Telephone _____

   Address: _____

   2nd Choice: _____ Telephone _____

   Address: _____

3. At death, please notify the following:
   Name: _____ Telephone _____

   Address: _____

   Name: _____ Telephone _____

   Address: _____

   Name: _____ Telephone _____

   Address: _____

4. My preference (if any) for a funeral director:

   _____

5. I have arranged for the gift of my body, or any part
   of it, to the following institutions: _____
   _____
   _____
   _____

6. ☐ I prefer immediate cremation without
   embalming, viewing or procession.
   ☐ I prefer immediate burial in a modest casket
   without viewing.
   ☐ I prefer other arrangements, as outlined:

7. I wish to be buried in the cemetery named below:
   _____

   The cemetery deed is located: _____

   Location of my grave in lot: _____

   Type of grave marker preferred (if any): _____

8. I desire a Funeral Service to be held at:
   ☐ Funeral Home
   ☐ Church
   ☐ Graveside Only
   Pastor desired: _____

   If unavailable, please contact Reverend: _____

   Readings and Scriptures: _____
   _____
   _____

Hymns to be Sung: _____
_____
_____

Viewing Requested:
☐ Yes
☐ No
Please note these special requests for the Funeral
Service: _____
_____
_____

I would like a Graveside Service:
☐ Yes
☐ No
Pleae note these special requests for the Graveside
Service: _____
_____
_____

The Graveside Service is for Family Only:
☐ No
☐ Yes
Pallbearers: _____
_____
_____

I desire ☐, I do not desire ☐ a Memorial Service in
the church after burial or cremation.
If a Memorial Service is held, the minister or
speaker should be: _____

Music desired for the Memorial Service: _____
_____

Readings of Scripture should include: _____
_____
_____

9. In lieu of flowers, I request that memorial gifts be
made to: _____ Church

or _____

10. This is information which may be needed on death
certificate or for use in the newspaper:
Date of Birth _____ Place of Birth _____

Citizenship _____ Occupation _____

Full Name of Spouse (including maiden name) _____

Father's Full Name _____

Mother's Full Name (including maiden name) _____

11. Here is a brief biographical sketch which can be
used by newspaper(s): _____
_____
_____
_____
_____
_____

*We, who are members of the family of the signer of this
STATEMENT, will do our best to carry out the provisions
listed above.*
Signature: _____ *Relationship* _____

Signature: _____ *Relationship* _____

Signature: _____ *Relationship* _____

Signature of Signer: _____

Date: _____

Resurrection Music For The Funeral Service

Gerald J. Wise

Funeral Service Hymns [for singing or hymn preludes]
"Hymns . . . do keep alive the religion of those who can learn to sing them from the heart . . ." wrote Winfred Douglas, in his scholarly treatise, *Church Music in History and Practice*. The twelve hymns listed below possess a vigor necessary to nourish and sustain spiritual life. They are not found under *Funerals* in the topical index of most hymnals, but are categorized — alive and well — under the headings "Hope", "Praise", "Providence", "Resurrection" and "Saints":

TITLE	*TUNE*
"A Mighty Fortress Is our God	Ein' Feste Burg
"Alleluia! Sing to Jesus"	Hyfrydol
"Christ, the Lord, Is Risen Today"	Llanfair
"For All the Saints"	Sine Nomine
"He (All) Who Would Valiant Be"	St. Dunstan's
"Hope of the World, Thou Christ of Great Compassion"	Donne Secours
"If Thou But Suffer God to Guide Thee"	Neumark
"Lord of All Hopefulness"	Slane
"O God, Our Help"	St. Anne
"Praise, My Soul, the King of Heaven"	Praise, My Soul
"Thine Is the Glory"	Judas Maccabaeus

An extraordinary degree of sympathy and unity arises as People of God share their common heritage through the singing of hymns. Hymn singing is a cathartic . . . a subtle reliever of emotional tensions.

Webster defines *catharsis* as: "a purification of the emotions that brings about spiritual renewal." I believe singing the *best* hymns the Church has to offer *can* bring about a spiritual renewal during the occasion of the Funeral Service.

Organ Music

Yet, in addition to providing the grieving community with catharsis and spiritual renewal, the element of music should also foster a sense of confidence . . . a period for reflection. The character of this confidence is revealed in one of the most poignant moments in Bach's spiritual life. It occurred as the blind and partially paralyzed cantor dictated his last chorale prelude to a former pupil, Christoph Altnikol. Bach had composed an organ setting of the melody, "When In The Hour Of Utmost Need," in his youth, but for this, his final affirmation of faith, he instructed Altnikol to write: "Before Thy Throne, My God, I Stand" (both texts were commonly sung to the same tune). Confidence. It is this confidence which music must reflect during the Funeral Service.

The list of suggested organ preludes encourages such quiet reflection and instills a sense of confidence. It forms a finely-drawn contrast with the virile hymn tunes noted above.

Composer/Title	Volume/Publisher

Bach, J. S.

Before Thy Throne, My God, I Stand — *The Church Organist's Golden Treasury Vol. 3* [O.D.C.]*

Blessed Jesu, at Thy Word — *The Liturgical Year (Orgelbuchlein)* [O.D.C.]*

Hark! A Voice Saith, All Men Are Mortal — *The Liturgical Year (Orgelbuchlein)* [O.D.C.]*

In Thee, Lord, Have I Put My Trust — *The Liturgical Year (Orgelbuchlein)* [O.D.C.]*

Jesu, Joy of Man's Desiring — *The Church Organist's Golden Treasure Vol. 3* [O.D.C.]*

Lord Jesus Christ, Be Present Now — *The Liturgical Year (Orgelbuchlein)* [O.D.C.]*

Our Father in the Heaven Who Art — *The Liturgical Year (Orgelbuchlein)* [O.D.C.]*

Brahms, J.

Blessed Ye Who Live in Faith Unswerving — *Eleven Chorale Preludes* [Mercury]

O God, Thou Faithful God — *Eleven Chorale Preludes* [Mercury]

O, World, I How Must Leave Thee — *Eleven Chorale Preludes* [Mercury]

Bridge, Frank

Adagio in E Major — [B.M. - H.W.G]*

Buxtehude, D.

Now, Holy Spirit, We Pray to Thee — *Treasury of Early Organ Music* [Mercury]

Darke, Harold

Chorale Prelude on "St. Peter" — *Three Chorale Preludes* [Novello]

Drischner, Max
If Thou but Suffer god to Guide Thee — Chorale Preludes for Organ (Or Harmonium) [C.L.S. - M.T.]*

Elmore, Robert
Chorale Prelude on "Seelenbrautigam" — Modern Anthology Part 2 [B.M. - H.W.G.]*

Oldroyd, George
My Soul Hath a Desire and Longing to Enter into the Courts of the Lord — Three Liturgical Improvisations No. 1 [Oxford]

Peeters, Flor
Aria — [Heuwekemeijer - Amsterdam] Ten Chorale Preludes Volume 1 [Peters]

O God, Thou Faithful God

Vaughan Williams, Ralph
Rhosymedre — Three Preludes Founded on Welsh Tunes [St. & B.]*

Vierne, Louis
Prelude in C Minor — French Masterworks for Organ [B.M. - J.F.B.]*

Walther, Johann
Lord Jesus Christ, Be Present Now — The Church Organist's Golden Treasury Volume 2, Var. 6 [O.D.C.]*

Publishers Key:

O.D.C. = Oliver Ditson Company
B.M. - H.W.G. = Belwin Mills — H. W. Gray Division
C.L.S. - M.T. = C. L. Schultheiss-Musikverlag-Tubinger
B.M. - J.F.B. = Belwin Mills — J. Fischer Bros. Division
St. & B. = Stainer and Bell